The
PORTABLE
PHD

The PORTABLE PHD

Taking Your Psychology Career Beyond Academia

Patrick Gallagher *and* Ashleigh Gallagher

AMERICAN PSYCHOLOGICAL ASSOCIATION

Washington, DC

Published by
American Psychological Association
750 First Street, NE
Washington, DC 20002
https://www.apa.org

Order Department
https://www.apa.org/pubs/books
order@apa.org

In the U.K., Europe, Africa, and the Middle East, copies may be ordered from Eurospan
https://www.eurospanbookstore.com/apa
info@eurospangroup.com

Typeset in Charter by Circle Graphics, Inc., Reisterstown, MD

Printer: Sheridan Books, Chelsea, MI
Cover Designer: Beth Schlenoff

Library of Congress Cataloging-in-Publication Data

Names: Gallagher, Patrick (Behavioral scientist), author. | Gallagher, Ashleigh, author.
Title: The portable PhD : taking your psychology career beyond academia/
    Patrick Gallagher and Ashleigh Gallagher.
Description: Washington, DC : American Psychological Association, [2020] |
    Includes bibliographical references and index.
Identifiers: LCCN 2019035676 (print) | LCCN 2019035677 (ebook) |
    ISBN 9781433831256 (paperback) | ISBN 9781433831720 (ebook)
Subjects: LCSH: Psychologists—Vocational guidance. | Psychology, Applied.
Classification: LCC BF76.G35 2020 (print) | LCC BF76 (ebook) |
    DDC 150.23—dc23
LC record available at https://lccn.loc.gov/2019035676
LC ebook record available at https://lccn.loc.gov/2019035677

http://dx.doi.org/10.1037/0000170-000

Printed in the United States of America

10 9 8 7 6 5 4 3 2 1

We dedicate this book to Hope, our favorite collaboration, with love.

Contents

Acknowledgments

We sincerely thank the professional psychologists who shared their personal experiences and thoughts with us. Our conversations with them have enriched and shaped our ideas and made this book a more valuable resource for readers.

We are grateful to faculty mentors who encouraged us to develop these resources for graduate students, and to Gigi Payne, who helped us find some quiet time to do so.

We owe a great debt of gratitude to Linda McCarter; the team at the American Psychological Association; and especially our editor, Susan Herman, who have assisted and supported this work at every step. Your patience and guidance have made realizing this book a pleasure.

Finally, we thank our loving families, M.B.G., and W.F.S., for unconditional support throughout our graduate school years, professional lives, and the writing of this book.

The
PORTABLE
PHD

INTRODUCTION

In talking with psychology graduate students and professors in recent years, we have noticed that many students have started considering increasingly diverse options for careers. Students and professors have been looking for information about how to prepare themselves or their students to pursue careers outside of academia. Indeed, employment trends indicate that many new doctoral degree holders are not working in academia: In 2016, among those PhD recipients in psychology and social sciences who had employment commitments upon graduation, 54.2% had secured academic positions, 20.2% had government or nonprofit positions, and 19.1% had positions in industry or business (we do not know about the employment situations of those without commitments; National Center for Science and Engineering Statistics, 2017). Unfortunately, we have also increasingly come across articles and blogs expressing dissatisfaction with the state of PhD training and careers (e.g., Schuman, 2014).

In our conversations, we wondered why many of the smart, hardworking, creative people who pursue PhD training and other advanced degrees in psychological science have trouble finding fulfilling work in the nonacademic

http://dx.doi.org/10.1037/0000170-001
The Portable PhD: Taking Your Psychology Career Beyond Academia, by P. Gallagher and A. Gallagher

world. Perhaps they are not looking hard enough, or not looking in the right places to find these jobs. Because we are social psychologists, however, we looked to the social context to understand what was really going on. Social contexts are often such well-known water that the fish forget it is there. How has PhD training not prepared students for nonacademic work? Why do potential employers fail to see what social scientists can contribute to their team?

We also noticed how many psychologists were graduating each year, and how many fewer tenure-track positions were open for all those newly minted PhDs to compete for. We heard from professor friends that search committees for open positions would receive applications from several hundred highly qualified people for a single open tenure-track faculty position. More and more PhDs seemed to be finding themselves, after grinding through 9 or 10 years of college and graduate school, with disappointing academic career prospects on top of relatively little preparation for nonacademic careers. How have so many early career PhD psychologists arrived at this situation?

We combined our analysis of the situation with our own and our colleagues' experiences bringing behavioral science to jobs outside the academy. We began taking note of what nonscientists understand, and do not understand, about our skills. We started to think about how best to capture nonscientists' attention when we wanted to propose or explain something. We also started noting the techniques that seemed to work when we successfully convinced people of the value that our skills or our social science expertise can add to policy, health care, and business applications. We began noticing, and defining, what worked and what did not work for communicating with potential employers, funders, partners, and teammates.

The next step was to break down what was underpinning the patterns we observed. What is it that stands in the way of effective communication between psychologists and others, and what has been lost in translation? What are the mechanisms preventing so many psychological scientists from fitting in outside academia? How do we overcome these obstacles? The answers to *these* questions, we thought, are what graduate students *really* need to know. We had both seen and heard successful scientists outside academia describe the paths they followed to their careers, and the ways they used their skills in their jobs. (We even described our own paths to inquiring students.) But those stories, we felt, were not generalizable because they did not equip the person with a solid, comprehensive strategy for preparing his or her own personal pursuit of nonacademic careers.

Psychological scientist. We use the term *psychological scientist* or *independent scientist* to refer to doctorate-level psychologists with research training. Notably, outside academia some do not understand or pay close attention to psychologists' credentials and refer to anyone with graduate training in psychology as a scientist. We feel that in some contexts, it is helpful for doctoral degree holders to refer to themselves as *independent research scientists*, because that can help others quickly understand that you (a) are not a therapist and (b) have research training just as a biologist or chemist research scientist does.

In recent years, more resources have appeared for psychology graduate students interested in nonacademic, or alternative-academic ("alt-ac"), careers. These include lists of jobs in which psychologists can work, inspiring stories from individual psychologists who have made careers outside academia, and specific guidance on how to prepare job application materials and develop interview skills. These resources are extremely valuable and certainly help graduate students build important skills and materials. But even they, we think, do not address the fundamental barriers that hinder many psychological scientists in career searches.

After several years of observation and analysis, we have gathered our ideas into a resource that, we hope, addresses those deeper fundamental barriers. Our goal is to provide guidance on examining your own set of knowledge, skills, and abilities; identifying careers that might interest you; preparing to pursue those careers; and being successful once you begin.

THE PREMISES APPROACH

The premises approach is our way of identifying, organizing, and providing guidance for navigating those hitherto unarticulated obstacles to nonacademic careers. We define *premises* as beliefs, attitudes, or habits that permeate the profession of academia that students are explicitly taught or simply absorb through the course of their doctoral training. A more formal definition of a premise could be a *postulate*, defined by the *Merriam-Webster.com Dictionary* as "a hypothesis advanced as an essential presupposition, condition, or premise of a train of reasoning" (Postulate, n.d.). We use *premises* instead of *postulates* to include less formal or defined constructs like attitudes. We believe that acting on premises without awareness of their implications is at the core of the difficulty psychological scientists encounter when they try transitioning to the nonacademic world. Premises are usually seen as the assumptions or facts upon which arguments are made or cases are built. Our conceptualization of premises fits with this idea—they underlie the decisions, judgments, attributions, and explanations we make.

Our definition of *premises* is not a scientifically precise one; we have no intention of proposing such a definition and building a theoretical case for it! It is simply a way of referring to a collection of phenomena that make up those hidden barriers.

Important to note, we do not believe that academic premises are wrong. We do not propose any judgment of the value or validity of a set of premises. Any training, especially one as intense and deep as PhD training, can deeply engrain ways of looking at the world that are different from the average person's. These new ways of looking at the world are in fact a necessary part of the training—for example, in the case of scientific training, students are trained to think in terms of hypothesis testing and probability, which is probably somewhat different from the way nonscientists think. Each professional field has such premises. The problems arise when one's set of premises is mismatched to others' premises or when one's premises obscure creative solutions to problems. Mismatched or obscuring premises can create hurdles to effective communication and translation of value from one field to another. The premises approach sets out to identify premises learned in academic training, explore when and how they act as hurdles for acculturation to nonacademic contexts, and provide a strategy for overcoming them.

In the rest of this book, we define many premises that might be useful to analyze in your nonacademic career pursuit. We provide guidance on preparing for your career journey not just with specific tips and techniques but also with a consideration of when and how premises might be operating. We think this is an effective lens through which to examine your qualifications and your career development because it addresses a crucial topic that has been missing from other sources of advice and provides principles that go beyond anecdotal experience—principles that anyone can apply to their own career path.

Before we get ahead of ourselves, we should pause to clarify how we are defining "academic" and "nonacademic" positions. They could be defined in many ways, but for the purposes of this book, we make this distinction based on workplace culture. Any position in an academic institution (a college or university) that involves teaching, where CVs are the norm, most employees have advanced degrees, and empirical research is a common language is probably an academic job. The classic example is a tenure-track professorship, but there are many other forms, such as non-tenure-track or contract positions that still require an advanced degree or ABD (all but dissertation). Administrative staff in an academic institution (such as offices of community outreach or research centers) will be familiar with the culture of academia, and so those positions are, for our purposes, also academic.

Nonacademic positions, on the other hand, are everything else. These are environments other than academic or basic research institutions. Hirers would not know how to interpret a CV and do not speak the language of empirical science or peer-reviewed publications. A good indicator of a non-academic job is when you are reading a job description and find yourself encountering language or terms wholly unfamiliar to you.

Many positions might be in the gray area between these two simplified groups—for example, a contract research organization might operate in many areas just like an academic institution. There are other possible ways to define academic versus nonacademic. The important thing is that different professional industries and contexts have different cultures, and different sets of premises that might not match those that prevail in your PhD training. If you understand that, you have a better chance of succeeding in any new job, no matter what industry or sector.

> **Hirer.** In this book we refer to anyone who might pay for your services as a *hirer*. They could be the manager who would be your immediate superior, the company to which you've applied, a potential investor, or a prospective client.

OUR STORY

Learning how to tell your own story will be an important part of your preparation for nonacademic careers, and we cover that process in Parts II and III of this book. By sharing our stories here, our purpose is to give you, the reader, a picture of who we are and where we have learned the lessons we discuss in this book. The following is a brief travelogue of the paths we have followed and created up to now. Because the rest of life can have a substantial bearing on how your career unfolds, we include a bit of the personal side of our journey too.

Ashleigh

I began college thinking I would major in English and attend law school, but I changed my mind when I took my first psychology course. I particularly loved social psychology and enjoyed assisting in research on culture and emotions during my time as an undergraduate. By the end of college, I knew I wanted to pursue a graduate education in experimental psychology.

I went on to earn my PhD from University of North Carolina at Greensboro. As a graduate student in social psychology, my research interests included social judgment, group processes, and aggression, and I received excellent mentorship from my faculty advisor. While a graduate student, I was a teaching assistant for a class in which Patrick was an undergraduate student, and this is how we met. Working together on a subsequent research project, we "fell in like" and started dating. By the time I finished my PhD program, Patrick was working on an MA in psychology and we had been a couple for a few years. I accepted a visiting assistant professorship, and we remained in the same geographic location until Patrick moved away for his PhD program.

I spent 2 years at Wake Forest University as a visiting assistant professor teaching undergraduate classes and supervising undergraduate research projects. During this time, I was considering pursuing the traditional academic path (i.e., research, teaching, service; publishing and thereby avoiding perishing), and this position provided me with a very positive and nurturing environment to try that career path on for size.

By chance, I saw a posting for a position applying social science to research and policy work in the court system of the state of North Carolina. I was very excited at the prospect of being able to apply my training to a context that had always interested me—the criminal justice system. I jumped at the opportunity and began this job while Patrick finished his PhD nearby. We married, I loved my new job, Patrick loved graduate school, and we both loved living together! For four years, I worked on a team of social scientists and attorneys contributing to research that informed policy decisions on felony and misdemeanor sentencing in our state. As a part of my job, I communicated research methodologies and findings to people from various backgrounds, including attorneys, judges, and state legislators. This time was marked by many valuable learning experiences; it took me a while to make the transition from academia to the applied world of policy-making, but teammates at work helped. We did not articulate it at the time, but I was getting on-the-job experience working through and around premise mismatches.

During this time, we also welcomed our daughter to the family and navigated major illness. When Patrick accepted his job in the financial services industry, it meant a move for us. I accepted a 1-year appointment as a lecturer at the University of North Carolina at Greensboro. I have just finished my 7th year in this role (now that of senior lecturer). I am currently the director of undergraduate studies for our department, I coordinate the academic advising system and direct the internship program in our department, and I teach a variety of classes that I love. I have been surprised by how much I genuinely enjoy mentoring students on the more practical aspects of their career.

The psychology departments I have worked in as well as my policy research position each had fulfilling and interesting missions. Each also provided me with the opportunity to represent my field and the knowledge it offers—be it to students or to other professionals.

Patrick

I started at the University of North Carolina at Greensboro as a media studies major, but when I took a biopsychology class I was hooked on psychology, eventually earning a second BA degree. During my junior year I took a group dynamics course, most notable for the beautiful graduate student teaching assistant who led our lab section, in whose lab I signed up to work, and whom I started dating.

I was then accepted to Wake Forest University's masters in experimental psychology program, where I focused on personality psychology. After Wake Forest I attended Duke University's social psychology program, where I continued studying personality processes, self-regulation, and decision-making. Ashleigh remained in the Greensboro area at first, but during this time she moved into her state government position, and we were married and lived together. At the end of my time at Duke we bought a house—in fact I defended my dissertation and we closed on our house the same day. As Ashleigh mentioned, 2 months later our daughter was born—it was an eventful time!

Near the end of my time at Duke, I began applying for tenure-track positions and received little interest. I was accepted to a postdoctoral research fellowship in behavioral health at the Durham VA Medical Center. This position was my first experience—a crash course, really—in applying my scientific training in a nonacademic environment. Figuring out how to communicate to patients, doctors, and nurses to make some difference with my science was a new challenge.

My next position was in the financial services industry, and our family moved once again after Ashleigh found her lecturer position. My job ended up morphing into four different jobs over time. First, I and a team of a few other psychology PhDs were tasked with figuring out how behavioral science could improve customer service and other operations at a business that was mainly a call center operation. Second, after about 6 months and under a new management team, we were asked to figure out how to systematize applying behavioral science to customer service. After about a year, we moved into a third area: marketing and market research. We were trying to figure out how to organize potentially useful scientific findings into a system we could apply to marketing campaigns to improve results. We soon transitioned into a start-up type of atmosphere, trying to build new products and businesses around them. The proposed products generally took the form of software or software-as-a-service that would use machine learning and psychological principles to improve customer communications and/or marketing campaigns.

We then transitioned back to a pure consulting model with a defined role—optimizing communications. My team would be hired to work on a certain marketing campaign, or scripts for call centers, and manage the relationship with the client as well as apply our science to improve the communications. Throughout my time at this position, I was involved in many interviews and hires, many for psychology-oriented jobs. I also supervised two summer internships for undergraduate psychology majors.

At my next position, my role was internal corporate communications. It was strictly applied work—I applied the best practices for using behavioral science in communications and customer experience that my earlier teams had developed. This position included ghostwriting for a top-level executive.

In my current position at a leadership consulting firm, I do many of the things that industrial/organizational (I/O) psychologists traditionally do. I measure the impact of the training programs, develop instruments, and advise based on relevant research literature. I design, administer, and report employee engagement surveys for several client companies. I design and carry out studies and provide consulting to functions such as employee training and recruiting and hiring. I supervise another PhD psychologist and collaborate with academic researchers and students on research projects. Finally, I develop products and services based in psychology research findings.

In addition to these positions, I have led or assisted others in small side ventures. For these projects, I have developed business plans, marketing materials, and funding applications. I have also done product development and market research. The skills I built in my PhD training are indispensable to my position. I feel as if I am putting that training to use to make a substantive contribution to my own and client companies and, more important, to help make many people's lives at least a bit better.

To sum it all up, in our combined 12 years in the applied/professional world and 9 years in university teaching, we have been fortunate to be exposed to quite a wide range of experiences. It is important to note that the explicit goal of several of our professional roles has been to convince others of the value of science findings or to design products or services based in our science. Those roles taught us how diverse audiences perceive academic science and how to identify what potential customers, employers, or clients find compelling. In addition, we have worked for people who did not necessarily set out to hire a PhD, and so it has been necessary for us in many contexts to explain or demonstrate what value we can bring, or indeed why we were even there. Our learning from those experiences culminated in this book and the premises approach to preparing for a non-academic career.

That is the story of how we arrived at the current coordinates on our own map. We think it is important to share our journey because it describes the experiences that have informed and shaped our ideas. Our psychology training and our careers thus far have been interesting, fun, sometimes challenging, and very fulfilling. Neither of us would trade our PhDs or our graduate school years for anything. Our training and psychology knowledge make up a good part of each of our identities and have helped us succeed in our career paths.

Sharing our story is also important because it illustrates that although a career path can seem linear and deliberate when described on a CV or résumé, life can take many twists and turns, and unexpected shifts in opportunities, interests, and priorities can change your course. Where you are in 10, 20, or 50 years will be the result not only of the career choices you make but also of circumstances you cannot know yet.

WHAT THIS BOOK IS

This book is intended as a guidebook for anyone who is entertaining the notion of transitioning from academia to an applied field. Just as any guide to a new culture would do, we provide you with inside tips to help make the relocation to your new culture easier and more successful. In our own forays outside academia, we wish someone who had navigated this transition could have helped us avoid some of the pitfalls and detours. This book attempts to fill that role—it provides tips and insights you might not get anywhere else.

We have set out to create a straightforward, practical resource that any psychology graduate student or PhD holder can use. We refer to *PhDs* and

PhD degree holders in the book title and throughout the book, but we hope to share information that is useful for anyone who holds or is working toward an advanced scientific or research-related degree. We aim to provide a resource that will help you to prepare for, and successfully transition to, a nonacademic career. We hope you will keep this book on your shelf and refer to it now and then through your graduate school journey, always keeping an eye toward preparing yourself for the widest possible range of career opportunities. Understanding the messages in this book can help you, as a psychology student, experience and interpret each aspect of your training through a new lens—one that will, if you decide to pursue a nonacademic career, enable you to build a compelling case to potential hirers.

We do not claim to have all the answers, and we encourage you to take advantage of any resource you can find online, from professional organizations, from your department, or other groups. But we believe that what we have captured in this book is unique.

This book is deliberately *not* a scientific research report, nor is it a review of the scientific literature on the experiences of psychologists leaving academia (to our knowledge, little if any systematic research exists on this topic). We do devote some pages to the psychological mechanisms that might underpin premises and their operation, and we cite research in that chapter. We also reference other sources of thought or experience that help illustrate or define some points. By and large, though, we avoid theoretical discussions. We want this book to be easy to read and reference. Consider it a change of pace from the dozens of research articles you are probably reading each week!

This book is also not intended to argue for one or the other type of career (academic vs. nonacademic). Both paths offer fulfilling, well-paying careers. Our goal is to aid transition between the contexts, which necessitates comparing and contrasting. That should not be taken as an endorsement or judgment of either over the other. (Indeed, one of us is currently in an academic job, and one is in a nonacademic job.)

And finally, this book is not a step-by-step instructional guide to building a résumé, finding job listings, how to network, and so on. In other words, we do not provide explicit instructions for carrying out all the steps of a job search. Comprehensive, valuable resources for those things are already out there, many are free, and we reference many of them throughout the book. Instead we have set out to write a book that provides advice specifically for people who are interested in transitioning from academic psychology to another sector. This book should be a companion to all the other resources you use to search for and apply to jobs. We have gathered ideas, experiences, and (a little) research that we think can broaden psychologists' horizons and streamline their careers. We wanted to offer material that can't be found anywhere else.

In advising students how to pursue nonacademic jobs, we have concluded that there is, unfortunately, not a one-size-fits-all list of possible jobs and how to get them (a list of possible career paths can be informative, however, and we refer you to Urban & Linver, 2019, for a useful list). We believe that each individual will need to build her or his own unique list based on their specific skills and interests and will have to learn through trial and error what works and does not work for their particular skills and experience and chosen career field. Moreover, such a list would be continuously changing, considering today's rapidly evolving professional landscape. This book does, however, include concrete strategies and action steps to begin your own personal prospective jobs list and plan out what you'll do to pursue one or more of them.

WHO CAN BENEFIT FROM THIS BOOK

Anyone in an academic career path considering a pivot—whether still training, in an early career position, or even later in a career considering a change—can learn something useful from this book. We focus on graduate students and postdocs, but the material is easily applicable to any stage of an academic career.

Several subfields of psychology, including clinical/counseling, school psychology, sports psychology, industrial/organizational (I/O), and many PsyD programs, include practical career training. Indeed, many such programs require students to complete a practicum or internship in an applied position. Such programs often prepare students for very clear career paths. Nevertheless, some psychologists might find alternative career paths very interesting and want to make a shift but do not know how to prepare. We believe this book can provide valuable guidance in that case.

If you are reading this, you are likely at least considering pursuing a nonacademic career. However, some readers might be reading out of curiosity, or to see if there is anything in this book that might be useful to them in their academic career. As for the latter, we believe that, yes, a good deal of the skills, strategies, and professional development advice we lay out will help you in pursuing an academic career. We provide advice and suggested courses of action that can help you articulate what you have to offer, communicate your skills, and be prepared to answer tough questions in any interview or other professional situation.

We suggest that even if you are not interested in nonacademic careers now, you might find that interest shifting over the course of your studies. We know many people who trained as scientists with a laser focus on becoming professors, only to be disappointed with their career options when they finished training. We would like to think we can help others in that situation, which is a chief reason for this book. It is a good idea to prepare yourself now for the possibility that your interests might shift over time. Reading this book and practicing a few of its suggested activities over the course of your training will go a long way to prepare you to hit the ground running if you do decide to look in alternative directions. Of course, if your intention all along has been to land a nonacademic job, this book is for you! We hope to provide a resource that can fill some gaps in your training.

OVERVIEW OF THE BOOK

First, we offer a three-semester self-guided development program that can help you start your preparation for a nonacademic career. In Part I of the book (Chapters 1 and 2), we delve deeply into premises. We define some core premises of academia that could be acting as barriers, discuss how they might be operating, and begin to explore ways to actively counteract those premises that can limit the scope of your career search or hold you back in hiring scenarios. In Part II (Chapters 3–5), we discuss the skills that PhD scientists have, and, through the premises approach, provide guidance on new ways of understanding and articulating your skill set. In Part III (Chapters 6–8), we discuss product development as a way to approach reconceptualizing not only your qualifications but also your career goals and purpose. In Part IV (Chapters 9–11), we provide strategies for searching for possible careers and forging your own unique career path.

In each chapter you will find one or more shaded boxes in which we define terms that are commonplace in many professional settings. Many of them are from the business world but are also well understood in other settings like policy or health care. To an academic they could seem buzzy or unclear, but they can be very important—they are shorthand that can go a long way toward breaking through mismatched premises and facilitating effective communication between you and potential hirers. We also use these boxes to define terms as we use them when they might be used differently elsewhere.

In each chapter we provide activities that help illustrate the chapter's concepts or help you start working on the ideas in the chapter. The What to Do Now exercises are meant to be concrete steps you can use to put the ideas and guidance in this book into action. They lay out useful activities that will help you understand what premises are, help you see how they might be working to complicate your career search, and help you work around them to build a strong set of career search materials and skills.

Psychological science has a lot to offer the world. Psychologists have uncovered fundamental properties of human functioning, and the value those findings can bring to the world is only partly realized. More psychological scientists should be out there, applying our science to improve people's lives. We know they can do it—we know *you* can do it! We offer this book in an effort to help make the transition from academia to non-academic life a little easier.

CAREER DEVELOPMENT TIME LINE

If you are not yet finished with your PhD training and have an interest in nonacademic careers, it can be difficult to block out time for career prep. We provide this time line as a suggested schedule.

We recommend that you start your career development plan as early as possible. The earlier you start, the more ground you can cover while you are still in graduate school. You might even be able to start developing a client base, building a track record, or making money, if those are goals you'd like to pursue.

If you are getting started early enough, each of the following time line sections can be expanded from one to two semesters. Of course, if you have less time than that, they can be condensed. We recommend, however, that you make a schedule, set goals, and hold yourself to them.

If you are finished with your PhD training, you can use the following time line as an overview or organizer of the information in this book. Work through each step at a pace that serves your career goals.

http://dx.doi.org/10.1037/0000170-002
The Portable PhD: Taking Your Psychology Career Beyond Academia, by P. Gallagher and A. Gallagher

FIRST SEMESTER: PREMISES AND SKILLS

1. First, read this entire book. It is important to understand the full scope of the ideas and strategies herein so you can work on the preparatory actions with the end goals in mind.

    a. While you are reading the book in your spare time, track the hours you spend on your studies each day. For at least 2 weeks, record every hour that you spend "at work" (attending class, studying, reading articles, preparing studies, gathering data, analyzing data, etc.). There are many free apps and software tools for tracking time spent on different categories of work.

    b. Analyze how you spend your time, and plan how much time you want to spend on nonacademic career preparation per week or month. Many time-tracker apps will have reporting capabilities built in to help you with this.

2. Next, work through each of the What to Do Now exercises in Part I. Do them honestly, and put in enough time to discover something about yourself or about how premises might be influencing your career pursuit.

3. Finally, work through the What to Do Now exercises in Part II. Again, spend enough time on them to generate good drafts of a résumé and a list of skills, informed by nonacademic people. Practice brevity, and practice describing findings in nonscientific terms while communicating the nuance and power or applicability of the findings.

    a. Brevity is a skill you should plan to continue practicing even as you move to the following semesters.

    b. The work you do in subsequent semesters will inform revisions of your résumé, list of skills, and the way you explain scientific findings, but at this point you are building a foundation.

4. We suggest spending the first month of the semester reading the book (of course, if you have the time to read it more quickly, all the better). Then you can spend 4 to 6 weeks (assuming a 4-month semester) on the second and third steps.

SECOND SEMESTER: PRODUCT DEVELOPMENT AND APPLICATIONS

5. Study Parts III and IV of this book. Complete the What to Do Now and in-chapter activities.

    a. If you find new lines of work that interest you, investigate them. For example, if you generate some ideas about how to apply research while working on the What to Do Now activity from Chapter 6, and you find yourself very interested in a certain field, continue reading about it and exploring organizations that work in that space. Note what you find, such as names of companies that are working in the area, the central sources of research that inform them, and your ideas about potential unmet needs you see.

6. Begin the process described in Chapter 11. Refine the résumé that you've drafted based on your Part III exercises, and post it on job sites. Create a profile, and apply to some jobs. Begin the process of selecting certain types of jobs, examining the types of listings the websites suggest to you, and studying the required skills in those listings. Research what the skills mean in those fields, and start forming ideas about where you might be most qualified. Start contacting recruiters and hirers.

   a. Even if you do not intend to actually take the jobs you apply to, apply anyway. You can learn about industries and the language they use this way. (If you happen to be contacted for an interview, be honest that you are interested in learning about the position but it would have to be a perfect fit or overwhelming offer for you to take it. There is no need to lead on a recruiter or hiring manager.)

   b. Use the new information you find to revise your résumé further. Start to draft different versions of it based on the different fields you are interested in.

   c. If you join a professional society that has a member directory, fill out your directory listing completely and subscribe to the job list, if applicable. Consider creating additional professional profiles on sites such as LinkedIn.

7. Continue attending nonacademic professional groups or events that you began in the previous semester. Begin cultivating a network of professionals and fellow students, and participate in it. Look for job leads, try out your content, and help others do the same.

8. As for timing, this semester's activities can be carried out simultaneously. You should complete the best résumé you can, but do not get bogged down trying to make it perfect. It will, in all likelihood, be revised many more times anyway.

THIRD SEMESTER: FINAL STEPS

9. By this time, you should have solid ideas about the direction(s) you want to take to pursue a career. In this semester, as you near the end of your training, it will be time to take bigger steps. First, if you have not

already done so, revise your résumé (or résumés) to be the best they can be based on the feedback and other information you have gathered. Now you should have a better idea of how to target them to the types of jobs you want.

a. Continue communicating with people you have contacted, especially those who showed interest in your qualifications or ideas. Contact them again now, and let them know your schedule for finishing your degree and any additional training.

b. If your goal is entrepreneurship, prepare a business plan and start pitching. If you feel it is not ready to present publicly, you can try to look for local events for proposals at your stage or informal sources of help, but it is important to get out there and start. This is the best way to learn how to improve your ideas.

c. If your goal is independent consulting, build a web presence and pursue clients. Contact consultants in your area, ask them for advice, ask for contract work, and generally seek help building a client base.

10. As you take these steps, of course, continue refining your résumé, proposals, or products based on the feedback you receive. Study Chapter 10 for ideas on how to build your own path.

PART **I** STARTING POINT:
ACADEMIC PREMISES

Any professional context has a set of beliefs, norms, assumptions, and attitudes. We refer to these collectively as *premises*. Some are explicit, some are never stated. Some are universally accepted by members of a given culture, others are not. Just as a traveler in a new culture would benefit from understanding differences between her home country and the new context, research psychologists seeking work in other fields will benefit from considering differences in premises.

We believe that understanding premises differences is a crucial component of successfully transitioning to a nonacademic career. Most graduate training programs, however, do not guide students to deliberately consider premises and adopt them. In the chapters in the Part I, we begin preparing you for your journey by placing premises at the center of the discussion. First, we define the term *premises* in more detail using some examples, and we develop the idea by considering when and how they might be at work in your context. Thinking about what premises you hold will allow you to move forward effectively with the guidance we offer on preparing and applying for nonacademic jobs.

1 ACADEMIA'S UNSPOKEN ASSUMPTIONS

In this chapter, we present what we have come to see as the most prevalent, the most impactful, and/or the least recognized premises at work in academic culture. We do not discuss all of them in depth here, but we refer to them throughout the book.

Before we present the list, we lay out some important implications and properties of the premises. Thoroughly thinking through what premises are is the first step to recognizing them and appreciating their potential effects in your career pursuits.

HOW PREMISES DEVELOP

If premises are attitudes, beliefs, ways of evaluating the world, values, or habits, then we presume they can be formed in the ways that any of those constructs are formed. As they form they can also become automatic—that is, not subject to conscious control, so that they operate in ways and on behaviors and decisions that are outside of your awareness. Knowing this,

http://dx.doi.org/10.1037/0000170-003
The Portable PhD: Taking Your Psychology Career Beyond Academia, by P. Gallagher and A. Gallagher

and knowing you are probably steeped in the culture of "the academy," what premises do you imagine are most prevalent in your thinking and behaviors?

Starting at the undergraduate level, students are taught how psychological researchers use the scientific method. Then, through methods courses, critical analysis of published research reports, and hands-on research training in graduate school years, students practice the assumptions and procedures that are necessary to conduct science until they are second nature. Such well-learned assumptions and procedures can easily make their way into the things you do outside the lab, even without any conscious decision to apply them. It is when premises are unconsciously exported from the lab and applied to new situations in the nonscientific world that complications can arise.

As an illustration, imagine you are at a party and you overhear a friend of a friend describe a troubling situation at work. She was selected to lead a high-profile marketing project, a rebranding of one of her company's products. She has spent 6 months planning it, and it is getting ready to launch. "Everything is riding on this," she says, "and if it fails I'll have nothing to show for all this work." You feel sorry for her, but it doesn't occur to you that your scientific training could offer a solution to her anxiety. But it can! Here's how: When you embark on a scientific study, the resources you devote to it are precious—there are only so many research participants, not much money, and limited time in your schedule. You would not set up a study that tests only a single hypothesis; you would include scales or capture dependent variables that allow you to test several secondary hypotheses (see Hedging Your Bets, in Chapter 4, this volume). This ensures that you get some value out of the endeavor, even if the main goal is not achieved.

You want to ask your acquaintance if she has any backup plans in case the marketing rollout isn't well received. How can she still have some results to show for all her good work? But instead you hold your tongue. You assume that she has thoroughly pilot-tested customers' reactions to the new branding and that secondary materials are prepared that might be used if needed. You hold back because of an implicit premise you espouse: pilot-testing and testing secondary hypotheses is a basic research skill. All scientists know how to do it. Therefore, it is not valuable enough to be featured or promoted.

Hedging your bets might not be a skill that you would think to discuss in a nonacademic setting, because of an implicit premise you hold, namely, that because it is a basic research skill, it is not novel enough to be of use. Suggesting this kind of approach and asking the right questions about how it could be applied, however, might resonate with your acquaintance at the party or perhaps impress an interviewer or client prospect.

THE NATURE OF PREMISES

Premises can come from several sources. They can be based in scientific training itself and therefore common to many different disciplines, or they can come from the general culture of academia, or they can even come from norms inside your specific subdiscipline. They can also have different effects. They can cause a breakdown in communication when two people's premises are mismatched, for example, or they can obscure your valuable skills that might appeal to potential employers.

As you begin to examine situations in which premises might be at work, thinking about the different sources and effects of the premises can be helpful. One of the main objectives of this book is to equip you to critically examine your own thoughts and habits to be more aware of if and how premises are operating. Simply thinking about where a premise might come from and the effects it can have might help you identify when they are operating; important to note, it also can help you adjust them to fit a new cultural context.

You should know several important points about premises. These points will help you objectively recognize them and make adjustments as needed to acclimate to your new environment.

- **Important Point #1: Do not abandon your academic premises.** We are not suggesting that the premises you have learned are wrong. In fact, we believe that some of them should indeed guide the academic researcher. We are certainly not suggesting you abandon them! Rather, we are pointing out that one should *be aware of them*, and be aware that outside academia, other people operate with different premises. Recognizing premises—not abandoning them, but taking them into account—is the key point in our approach.

- **Important Point #2: Not every academic holds all the premises.** In fact, many of the premises have been openly discussed as issues, and many academics dispel them. Nevertheless, they are still there—a part of the culture of department labs, seminar rooms, or national conferences. As stated in our upcoming list of academic premises, the premises might seem stark or extreme, but we contend that even if many people do not explicitly endorse them, their presence in the academic milieu still affects many students' attitudes, beliefs, and career preparations.

- **Important Point #3: No one is at fault for the premises.** By identifying some of the premises, we are not issuing criticism, because we do not believe anyone is setting out to do anything adverse. Instead, we believe that learning the premises is just a part of academic cultural transmission and some of the premises may in fact be relics from yesteryear. On the whole, we believe that advisors and graduate programs have the best of intentions and are doing everything they can think of to help students succeed.

- **Important Point #4: The economy of academia sustains the premises.** Like any other context, there are well-defined markers of success and powerful incentives for achieving those markers. Behaviors, attitudes, and beliefs that help people reach those markers are reinforced and become more frequent, so there is no avoiding that process and the resulting premises. The goal of this book is not to argue for change in that process; instead, we aim to equip the reader to know how to navigate new environments with new economies.

- **Important Point #5: The implicit nature of the premises makes their importance hard to appreciate.** Perhaps the sneakiest aspect of the premises is that many, if not all of them, become implicit and/or automatic. That aspect is why we think this guidebook is needed—it takes time and concentrated effort to spot these implicit assumptions and when they are at play.

ACADEMIC PREMISES

The following list provides a sample of the academic premises you may have learned in the course of your doctoral work.

- The scientific method, as taught in the psychology research tradition, is the single and ultimate standard for pursuing truth.

- Several citations must be behind a statement for it to be worthy of consideration.

- *Impact*, or contribution to society and the world, is defined by the number of citations, advancement of theory, grant dollars awarded, or publication in the right journals.

- Publishing research is the marker of success—funding for the institution and the individual researcher depends on research products; this is where the adage "publish or perish" comes from.

- Teaching is a lower priority than research, and success affords one the opportunity to opt out of teaching.

- The more advanced and complex research designs and more advanced statistical tests used, the better the researcher and the more valuable the research results.

- If your research is good enough, you will succeed on its scientific merit alone. Similarly, if you are willing to work hard enough and long enough, you will succeed in academia.

- New and counterintuitive research questions are more valuable than replication studies (notwithstanding the recent replication crisis).

- Research that breaks new ground, ventures far from what is already known, and stakes out new positions is of the highest value.

- You have to make an *individual* name for yourself.

- Everyone knows and agrees on the most valuable skills and achievements an up-and-coming researcher should have.

- Identifying weakness in others' work and calling attention to them is a valued skill and an important habit for shaping your own work.

- Taking your research efforts out of academia (especially into a for-profit environment) is selling out.

- Applied work is of lesser value than theoretical research, and resorting to it means you have settled for something less or cannot cut it in academia.

These premises may sound extreme; some are. When asked, many advisors do not explicitly endorse them or will heavily qualify them. However, these basic rule-of-thumb premises are out there in the academic culture. The "culture" of a workplace, a field, or an in-group is defined by not only what individuals explicitly state as the rules or guiding principle but also how things are ultimately carried out in behaviors—all the small choices, evaluations, or judgments that are carried out day to day: The reviewer who prioritizes one symposium proposal over another because it is more counterintuitive. The professor who promotes a student who is getting interest from academic positions compared with the student who is not. The student who feels some resistance from her advisor when she expresses more interest in teaching undergraduates than in embarking on another research project. It is no surprise that after having experienced years of exposure to these subtle or not-so-subtle cultural forces, many graduate students have a set of ingrained premises that affect their career pursuits.

The main goal of this section was to define what we mean by premises and articulate some examples. We continue developing the idea of premises and providing examples throughout the rest of the book. We do hope, however, that this introduction will help you begin reflecting on the attitudes, beliefs, habits, and principles that underlie your approach to your career search or career change. We want to again emphasize that these attitudes, beliefs, and habits are not suggested or implied to be invalid. Instead, we want to encourage self-awareness of the premises you hold before you begin interacting with people from other workplace cultures.

YOU ARE HERE

Think of a map with a "You Are Here" dot. In planning the first steps toward preparing for a possible nonacademic career, we recommend that you first orient yourself by mulling over the premises we just listed. Think about where they come from and the implications they might have for your career preparations. Also, consider the other points listed here about the nature of premises. Finally, start thinking carefully about your own assumptions and beliefs that might have been shaped by your academic training. How might they be playing out in your actions, your aspirations, and your long-term career goals? The What to Do Now section at the end of the chapter lays out some concrete suggestions for how to begin.

   Next, we discuss some ways that premises could limit your success outside the academic context and how you might counteract those possibilities. These processes will be very familiar to many psychologists. This chapter is surely not an exhaustive review; you may well identify other ways the premises can sneak up on you. The main point here is that some of the very topics we study in psychology can inform us about how the premises are influencing our behaviors when we venture out of the academy.

Your Critical Thinking Skills May Be Misunderstood

Academia has a distinct culture, and all cultures have *norms*, or accepted standards and prescriptions for appropriate social behaviors in situations. Many norms are never explicitly taught, and yet somehow people come to hold them dearly and strongly penalize those who violate them (Kahneman & Miller, 1986). For the sake of illustration, we revisit the familiar example of the proper behavior for riding in a public elevator. Although most parents will never formally instruct their children on elevator-riding procedures, we all successfully enter adulthood knowing to stand facing the elevator doors and keep our eyes directed on the number display with minimal social engagement.

Likewise, successful completion of a graduate degree in psychology requires mastering the culture's norms; it is an adaptive feature of group membership. Consider for a moment the normative behaviors for a 3-hour graduate seminar. Graduate students quickly learn that in their seminar classes, peer-reviewed and published science will be thoroughly examined (and critiqued) for its scientific rigor and soundness, its generalizability, and its implications. In this situation, the educational goal is to develop the independent thought processes of the emerging researcher. It is not uncommon to see graduate students in pursuit of that goal boldly offer their ideas on how the research could be improved upon or could have been better in some regard—for example, did the authors examine gender differences? In and of itself, the ability to critique work and offer new perspective or insight that advances science is a vital academic skill and a valuable one even outside academia. Over time, however, the focused and constant monitoring for the Achilles' heel of others' work can move from an exercise of constructive criticism to a general orientation of criticism, or worse, to others perceiving you as just plain critical. In work cultures outside academia, we must navigate the particular tension of being critical thinkers without being perceived as critical people. This can be especially tricky when we forget to adjust to the norms of a new context.

A fundamental feature of academic psychology is that science (i.e., knowledge) is built through disagreements that get fleshed out experimentally. Disagreements lead to empirical tests, and these tests, along with their data, conclusions, and theory revisions, build the science. Ultimately, paradigms may shift. We personally love that model and stand by it wholeheartedly; it is necessary for the growth of our knowledge of human behavior. However, without careful attention to the cultural norms of your new workplace, brandishing those critical-thinking skills in a way that adheres to the norms of academia can lead to frustrating interpersonal experiences. I (Ashleigh) was once informed in a nonacademic job performance evaluation that my teamwork skills needed some improvement. I was a little surprised by this specific criticism; after some reflection, I recognized that I had been approaching my team meetings as if they were lab meetings. With that mind-set, I had been eager to question assumptions, challenge the status quo, or play devil's advocate. In fact, I thought I was being a good and helpful team member by contributing in this way. Outside the culture of academia, however, my teammates experienced it as simply unsupportive or disagreeable. We were not operating with the same set of norms!

Your Goals May Limit Your Experiences

When we set goals for ourselves, we systematically filter out information deemed irrelevant to those goals, even before consciousness (Ansorge, Kiss, & Eimer, 2009). Without the active oversight of your conscious awareness, you may be missing out on things your brain has filtered out during perception. It is therefore a useful exercise to step back and reexamine the nature of the goals you have set for yourself. Let's say you find yourself talking to someone at a social or professional event. Your conversation partner is bemoaning the fact that at work, his supervisees are having trouble following a new regulatory change that the company has had to make. Because that practical problem sounds boring, too specific to that company, or atheoretical, it might slip right by you and not even pique your interest.

However, if you construe what you just heard as a question about how one can influence supervisees' behavior, you might suggest to your conversation partner that a social scientist could facilitate change management through several strategies, including (a) introducing improved communications to target attitude change, (b) conducting research to find root causes of resistance, (c) optimizing new processes to interrupt set habits and create new lasting ones, and (d) tracking and quantifying program success. In so doing, you might get yourself a lead on a well-paying job; at the very least, your interest and thoughtful insight have likely made a positive impression on a member of your social network. A careful examination of your premises could help broaden your goals and broaden your opportunities.

Your Attitudes Might Be a Problem

We all hold attitudes, and those attitudes are one important influence on our behaviors. Indeed, even implicit attitudes (those you might not recognize holding or be able to articulate) could be biasing your attention or behavior (Lundberg & Payne, 2014). The bias is reflected in the career possibilities you've considered or ruled out, or about the job applications you've submitted or those you've decided against. When you take your training outside academia, it is a good idea to spend some time intentionally considering the attitudes you hold. One of the premises we identified is that nonacademic jobs are inferior to academic—particularly tenure-track—positions (as expressed in Schuman, 2014; although of course not all academics endorse this view).

Although there is probably not too much harm in some in-group favoritism in this case, the marginalization of the out-group is unnecessary. Even if you do not endorse these attitudes, you might unwittingly adopt them to some degree, and they can subsequently affect the career options you consider or the training opportunities you take advantage of. They can keep you pursuing a job track that is not the best fit for you or that would make you less happy—all because you've internalized some negative attitudes about applied or industry careers from those around you. Just like your uncle Leo's job advice at holiday family gatherings is only *one* source of attitudinal influence on your career, so is Professor Leo's. Both have their value, and both have limits on their perspectives. The good news is that you will not have to surrender your smart card by moving outside academia, and there are many fulfilling ways to apply your psychological science skills to interesting questions out in the world. Many people putting their PhD to work outside academia feel that they wouldn't go back to academia if offered the chance (although that academic calendar *is* very tempting!).

Your Attributions May Be Fundamentally Erroneous

One of the attitudes just discussed—that nonacademic careers are inferior—can influence our explanations about people's career choices in a specific way. The *fundamental attribution error* (FAE), or correspondence bias, is our tendency to make internal or dispositional explanations instead of situational explanations when evaluating people's behaviors (Gawronski, 2004). (There is debate as to the mechanisms of this phenomenon and whether it is indeed fundamental, but we feel it is prevalent enough to discuss here.)

One frequently observed FAE is that people with PhDs who are working outside academia are doing so only because they were unsuccessful in academia. The attributional logic goes something like this: If a doctoral student is bright enough, works hard enough, and sacrifices enough, she will land a tenure-track position and eventually earn tenure. Stated in athletic coach terms, she has to *want it* badly enough. If that person has not worked hard enough, is not bright enough, or does not sacrifice enough, the nonacademic careers are there as a backup. It is ironic that psychological scientists fall prey to this error, but of course researchers are humans too! Although universities produce far more PhDs than they can place in tenure-track positions, we often demonstrate the FAE in our explanations of why someone took a nonacademic job. Several moderators can determine whether we make the FAE in this situation: how well we know (or like) the person who is discussed, the security or insecurity of our own career prospects, or whether the person is part of our ingroup.

We are all human, and to the extent that this error is fundamental, we are all subject to it; we can chalk it up to human frailty. The challenge for

PhD students considering career options is that oftentimes the very people advising us on career path choices are faculty members who have an academic position and who may communicate to us unwittingly that if we will do enough, we will succeed. Now, it is absolutely true that the tenure-track path requires hard work, many sacrifices, and bright intellect. Our point is merely that pursuit of an alternate career track does not require the absence of those characteristics. Frank discussions that center around chance factors are relatively infrequent. For example, which research topic will be "hot" the year you launch? How many jobs will be available in the year you go on the market? Will any of them be in a place you want to live? We do not suggest undue focus on these admittedly uncontrollable factors, but you might find yourself surprised by just how many of these uncontrollable chance factors there are. As such, you could probably benefit from asking advisors and mentors candidly about them.

You May Be *Under*thinking Things

There are well-known pitfalls in evaluating prospects and making decisions; as with the FAE just discussed, these errors and biases affect us researchers just as they do the participants in our studies. Psychological scientists Daniel Kahneman and Amos Tversky changed the way we think about thinking. Arguably, no other collective body of work in the field of psychology more definitively slayed the notion that we are "rational" thinkers than theirs. Here we mention only a few of their concepts as possible mechanisms for the premises. You can read more about their research in the fascinating book *Thinking, Fast and Slow* by Daniel Kahneman (2011).

Availability Heuristic

Let's face it, you spend your day surrounded by highly accomplished, highly intelligent people. After years of regular interaction and collaboration with such successful individuals, you may begin to take the inevitability of the tenure path for granted. Sure, we all know that the pursuit of tenure can be a gut-wrenching, harrowing experience, but almost all of the examples around us are of people who survived it, came out on the other side victorious, and lived to tell the tale.

The availability heuristic suggests that we tend to estimate the likelihood of an event based on the ease with which we can call to mind a ready example of it (regardless of base rate). Frequently used examples include the distorted estimates of airplane crash fatalities and automobile crash fatalities. Because virtually all plane crashes are newsworthy, whereas only a fraction of car crashes are, we overestimate the probability that we will fall victim to a plane crash and underestimate the probability that we will fall victim to a car crash. In both cases, we are neglecting the base rate of these occurrences.

Being mentored by successful and tenured professors might make it easy to believe that tenure is inevitable in one's own career. Of course, this distortion should be corrected. Doing so can help us make decisions that are realistic and informed by base rates.

Confirmation Bias

The *confirmation bias* is our tendency to notice and remember information that confirms our hypotheses and to disregard or discount information that counters or refutes our hypotheses. So, how are your premises working through confirmation bias? One way is that you may not notice or remember cues you are receiving from others who do not share your premises. The cues may fly right over your head unnoticed! At a certain point in our non-academic jobs, we were totally surprised to learn that some people hold negative stereotypes about PhD scientists and professors. It had honestly never occurred to us that a doctoral degree could in any way be a liability, except that people might expect us to wear tweed. To this day, it is still somewhat unimaginable to me that more education on a subject could seriously be viewed in a negative light.

Perceptions of PhDs and professors can be negative sometimes ("absent-minded" is one term that comes to mind). Others who work with doctoral degree holders can have a different perception of them than they do of themselves. We are still wholeheartedly in favor of earning the PhD, but after learning more about others' stereotypes of PhD scientists, we began to notice cues we had previously missed. We have become more sensitive to others' premises, taking care to try to disconfirm negative stereotypes. Left unchecked, however, the confirmation bias can perpetuate the influence of the premise on behavior, and interactions with others can suffer.

Bias Blind Spot

"I do not miss the pervasive attitude [in academia] that publications and funded grants are the predominant drivers for measuring success. It strikes me as not being too dissimilar from listening to people in sales functions bragging about their accounts." This quote from a psychology PhD we know who now works in business illustrates the bias blind spot—the difficulty of appreciating one's own systematic biases, even if you can spot them readily in others. The salesperson and professor might display the same behavior—judging each other's pride as misplaced—and not appreciate that their judgment is biased by their respective premises.

It can be hard to recognize and intercept biases. We sampled only a few of the many biases and heuristics that plague our social judgments, but we hope that one or two have resonated with you and provided a starting place for evaluating your own premises.

WRAP-UP

The main goals of this chapter were to define and list premises and to discuss some mechanisms for how they might operate. We do not expect you to have a full appreciation of premises and how they operate based on this chapter alone; we continue developing the idea and providing examples in the rest of the book. We want to reemphasize that we do not think these attitudes, beliefs, and habits are invalid—instead, we want to encourage self-awareness of the premises you hold as you venture out into new contexts. Like the "You Are Here" dot on a map, this chapter describes your current surroundings so you can successfully plot and navigate the course ahead.

As the first steps toward preparing for a possible nonacademic career, we recommend that you mull over the premises we listed. Whether you subscribe to them or not, how might they be playing out in your actions, your aspirations, and your long-term career goals?

TAKEAWAYS

- Every field has premises, and the reward structures and norms of the field shape the premises.

- Premises can be ideas or beliefs that are not explicitly taught or even endorsed but nevertheless become important factors that influence your behaviors.

- Several well-known psychological phenomena may help perpetuate premises and their effects.

- Cognitive biases likely make it difficult to recognize premises and when they are acting.

WHAT TO DO NOW

1. This exercise is meant to help you become more familiar with the premises, including gaining an appreciation of the different forms they can take. Remember, it is not necessary (or productive) to debate the merit of any premises.

   For each of the premises listed in this chapter, think about whether they originate in training in the scientific method or in the culture of professional academia more generally.

   Next, think about the following questions:

   a. Are any of them hard to classify (origins in scientific method vs. academia more generally)? Which could go into both categories?

   b. After reading and thinking about the premises presented earlier, do any other premises come to mind? Where might they have originated?

   c. For each premise, think about whether it is an attitude, a belief, a habit, or another construct. What does the nature of each premise suggest about how to recognize its presence, or how it might influence your judgments or behaviors?

2. This exercise is introspective. To get the most benefit from it, be open and candid with yourself.

   Think of graduate students you know or have heard about who did not follow an academic career track or did not follow the tenure track within academia. As you answer the following questions, write down everything that comes to mind. Give each question a few minutes' thought:

   a. What was the career path that led them to their current positions?

   b. What attribution do you make for why they have their positions, and what attribution do you make for why others you know have tenure-track faculty positions?

   c. What career path do you think they will follow over the next 5 years? 10 years?

Now, take a look back through your answers and see if you can find any premises at work. As you did with the previous exercise, think carefully about the things you normally do not examine. What are the beliefs that colored your opinions? What assumptions might have affected any evaluative thoughts?

2 CULTURAL ADAPTATIONS YOU'LL NEED TO MAKE IN YOUR NEW WORKPLACE

In this chapter, we discuss four examples of academic premises that are mismatched to premises in the nonacademic world. The chapter has two main goals: first, to examine a few more specific examples of premises and explain how they can cause complications in successfully navigating nonacademic career fields; and second, to illustrate the process of assessing premises and adjusting them. Working through these examples can help you appreciate the impact of the premises on your career search. Examining these premises might seem tedious at first, but with practice you will develop adaptive habits that will help you to be successful in your new work context.

The four examples in this chapter are broad and have readily identifiable consequences. In reality, some of your premises are more complex and might be more specific to your experience or your subarea of psychology. As such, their effects can be subtler. One of the premises we discuss likely originates in your training in the scientific method, two others probably come more from the culture of academia, and the fourth is actually a premise held *about* academics by others. All four could lead to communication failures, or they could obscure your skills that are valuable outside academia.

http://dx.doi.org/10.1037/0000170-004
The Portable PhD: Taking Your Psychology Career Beyond Academia, by P. Gallagher and A. Gallagher

PLACING HIGHER VALUE ON NOVEL RESEARCH FINDINGS

What kind of research findings are the most valuable? What studies attract the most attention or are the most useful? Which findings are more likely to be published or obtain grant funding? In many cases, the answer is new, groundbreaking, sometimes counterintuitive findings. As a new PhD, the way to make impact and build your career is to publish splashy, surprising new findings. Researching old, well-established processes or theories is somewhat less popular because there is a sense that "we already know that," and spending more time on it may imply a lack of creativity or originality.

There is, of course, good reason for valuing new and surprising research. Researchers *should* be expanding the boundaries of what we know. New discoveries are what advance basic science and, in turn, advance applications such as new medications or educational innovations. But this focus on the new and surprising has the de facto effect of devaluing explorations in older research areas, even when there are still open questions to resolve or unreplicated findings to confirm and build upon. This premium on the new and surprising is one of the factors implicated in the "replication crisis." This is, like many of the premises we explore, a result of the economy of the field. Up-and-coming researchers need to catch the attention of their peers to be competitive for tenure-track positions and grant funding as well as carve out their place in the field, and both can be accomplished with counterintuitive new findings. Thankfully, new outlets are opening for publishing replications, and organizations such as the Center for Open Science facilitate preregistration of studies and data sharing, even of nonsignificant results.

This is a good place to say, once again, that the purpose of this book is to recognize premises and account for them in your career search, not to debate their validity or root out who is responsible for them. Those are interesting topics, and they are being discussed in other forums, but your professional development time is probably better spent on making sure that premises are not hindering your success.

The Implication: Devaluing the Tried-and-True

What is the implication of this premise for your career or career search? Our main point is that outside academia, a disproportionate focus on the new and groundbreaking might lead you to miss many opportunities to solve problems or help people. If a 50-year-old finding can help solve a client's problem, then use it! Old research findings can be very valuable. In the applied context, they are not something to be avoided or treated as a "given"; instead, they can be the most appropriate, interesting, or valuable information to potential clients or employers.

There is accumulated wisdom in the things we have known for decades. Well-established, thoroughly replicated and tested psychological phenomena are perhaps the most valuable currency psychologists have. They may seem obvious when you are training to be a scientist, but they represent our field's greatest contributions to human knowledge. Brand-new counterintuitive findings, in contrast, are less developed and maybe even unreplicated. Even if they are the results of well-designed research, boundary conditions, modifiers, and mechanisms might not be fleshed out enough to reveal clues about how best to apply them outside a lab.

You might find it hard to resist talking about novel, flashy studies—people enjoy hearing surprising and powerful findings, especially if they are described compellingly in story form, as on a podcast. In some cases, then, it can be helpful to refer to new research findings to pique interest or to help call attention to well-established findings. It is important to realize, however, that when you move out of an environment full of psychology experts (academia) and into one filled with experts in other areas, most people have never learned what you learned in your first-year graduate seminars, or perhaps even in your upper-level undergraduate classes. Research that is less rewarded by your academic colleagues because it is so well known in our field can be useful, valuable, and even fascinating to others if it is explained and applied well. It is also important to keep in mind that well-educated, bright, thoughtful people are no less bright because they are unaware of basic findings in your particular science.

How to Adjust: Talk About the Basics

Do not hesitate to talk about the basics over and over again. To nearly every new person you meet outside academia, the most basic findings in your science will be unknown. Find compelling ways to demonstrate the basic, well-documented findings of your science, and use them again and again. (This is not unlike how you go about teaching a really great introductory-level undergraduate class.) You might think that repeating the old information would be boring—and it can be. It is energizing, however, when you can help someone apply that information to solve a problem or improve people's lives. Your work here may not advance a theory, but learning how to help people with a scientific fact can be a worthy and rewarding pursuit. Seeing policy, laws, or best practices change because you informed an audience about social science research is pretty satisfying.

PRESENTING RESEARCH METHODS

When it came time to present your first-year project, or your master's thesis, how did you spend most of your preparation time? What anticipated questions from the audience caused you the most trepidation? When you presented a poster at your first conference, or when you gave your first talk, what sections of your presentation had you practiced the most?

For many students, methodology and data analysis are the largest focus of study and preparation—and the biggest source of anxiety. This makes perfect sense: You are a novice being trained in the methods of conducting science, and precision in methodology and analysis is essential for reaching valid conclusions. As a student who is still learning the craft and gaining experience, you can justifiably be nervous about defending your methodology decisions. To finish your degree, in fact, you must literally "defend" your dissertation—to demonstrate in part your mastery of the methodology. A result of completing PhD training can be a habit of overanalyzing and overjustifying every detail of methodology and data analysis strategy.

The Implication: Obscuring Your Contribution

In a workplace setting, whether you are a traditional employee or a consultant, you might find yourself working with few or no other people who have the same training and qualifications that you do. Even if you are working on a team of scientists, perhaps on a research and development team, you might find yourself often communicating to a client or to leadership whose primary criterion for evaluating methodology is merely your affirmation that it is sound. That's pretty much it: Did you follow established best practices? Are you confident in these conclusions? If your answer to these questions is a simple yes, then your client or manager may well be satisfied.

> **Best practices.** *Best practices* are the methods or processes that are generally accepted to be the best, most effective way of doing something. They are normally specific to certain industries (e.g., best practices in ID verification in the online banking industry) or fields (e.g., best practices in candidate interviewing in the human resources field). When it comes to scientific methods, you will likely be the go-to authority on best practices. Notably, some current best practices will not be based on rigorous evidence. Challenging the received wisdom of best practices with evidence of a better way to do things is one way a research psychologist can bring value to an industry or an organization.

You might find that you are the person who was hired to evaluate and pass judgment on the soundness of research methodology—the subject matter expert. Indeed, there might not be anyone else in the organization who even knows how to question your method. You will probably not be asked, in other words, to justify why you used an oblique or an orthogonal rotation in your factor analysis, and if you told anyone, they would likely have no idea what to think. It might be an inherent part of your job to make those decisions based on your best judgment and simply deliver your conclusions. As you can imagine, this is a bit liberating!

> **Subject matter expert.** The *subject matter expert*, or SME (sometimes pronounced "smee"), is the person who is the authority in the company or on the team on some topic. If you are the only behavioral scientist in your organization, you will likely be the SME on behavioral science or research. If you are on a team of scientists, one of you might be asked to act as the research or psychology SME on a particular project or for a cross-functional team.

The implication of the premise that methodology must be exhaustively scrutinized, presented, and defended is that such a habit in an applied setting can distract, bore, and/or turn off an audience. This is almost incomprehensible to a social scientist, but remember that in your new context, the science is in the service of practical application. This is the difference between basic science and applied science. You can include your methodology in an appendix or a supplement, and of course you need to document your methods and keep them on file. But describing details of methodology or data analysis excessively or without being asked will often hamper the delivery of a valuable insight, finding, or recommendation; worse, it can even obscure the value you are bringing to your organization.

As an illustration, I (Patrick) routinely present survey findings to clients, and my habit now is to feature methodological details that are necessary for properly interpreting the results—for example, low response rates or sample sizes, notable demographic patterns, or new collection methods. I would make available, for example, the decisions I made while conducting a regression analysis, but they would not appear in the client presentation unless requested.

How to Adjust: Focus on the *Purpose* of Studies

We are not suggesting that you can be cavalier about methods or cut corners. Indeed, in most positions your name, reputation, and paycheck will depend on the soundness of your conclusions, which of course depends on the integrity of your methods. But you will not need to spend much time *talking about* methodology outside of your research team (if you have one). One adjustment to make in this area is to become comfortable not talking about each and every detail of the method. Your purpose in writing or talking about studies will be to inform decisions, not to enable the reader or listener to replicate your work, so it is not necessary to provide every detail. You still should be prepared to defend what you did and to replicate it yourself. But a straightforward determination of whether the methodology is sound is all most people will want to know, and you are probably the expert they have hired to take care of that. The most interesting and useful parts, to most clients or audiences, is the finding or conclusion and its implications for next steps.

THE IMPORTANCE OF BEING "IMPACTFUL"

Academic departments want to hire the most impactful researchers they can find. For research psychologists, one's impact in their field is also the biggest component of tenure decisions—along with teaching accomplishment and departmental service, often less important. Consequently, academia has several metrics by which to measure impact in the field, including number of publications, publications in top journals, and number of citations per publication.

The premise at issue here is that your professional efforts should be devoted to this type of impact. This is another example of a premise that makes a lot of sense: Many professional fields reward work that is judged as highly impactful by standards internal to that field. Professionals, including researchers, should aspire to such industry-specific contributions.

The Implication: Missing Alternate Measures of Impact

This premise can hinder a career search when it obscures attention to the other ways to measure impact. In your graduate and postdoc years, and into your pretenure professorship time, much, if not all, of your energy is justifiably focused on publications and other ways to establish professional impact. The risk of this focus is that it becomes the only impact you see as important.

What if you could count the number of people whose work life is more fulfilling because of your research? Or maybe the number of people whose perspectives have changed for the better because of your guidance? Or perhaps the improvement in profitability you bring to a company, which then allows them to employ more people who will provide for their families?

If these alternative measures of impact are important to you, the merits of some other career paths might become more apparent. It might be easier to consider a career outside of academia and easier to handle the subtle or not-so-subtle resistance from others to your considering such a career. One stark example of contributing to improving people's lives happened to me (Patrick): Partly because of the results of an employee engagement study that I conducted, one client company gave pay raises to much of their workforce.

In terms of a more specific implication, appreciating the possibility of other ways to impact the world can help you better communicate with people outside academia. Thinking of impact in these broader terms will likely resonate much more strongly with potential employers or other professional contacts who can help you acclimate to a new field. Indeed, many will not be familiar with the metrics that academia uses to quantify impact. We do not mean to suggest that your CV will be unintelligible outside academia—on the contrary, many potential hirers will certainly understand that publications are one of the marks of a successful scientist and will recognize that service to your field is a valuable achievement that speaks to your qualifications. But an applicant who is able to speak of impact in broader terms might have an advantage over one who prizes basic science accomplishment most.

One tenured professor once told us that he realizes his teaching will influence far more people than his publications ever will. This was not a novice or seldom-published professor—he in fact is very prominent and has published many books and far more than 200 scientific publications with about 45,000 citations. Unfortunately, most journal articles are rarely read, and virtually never by anyone apart from other scientists in your specific area of your subfield of psychology (Biswas & Kirchherr, 2015). In one sense, this doesn't matter so much; in the academic context, your career may not be affected by how many of your publications go unread by the outside world. Especially in the early stages of an academic career, unread publications still demonstrate your ability to navigate the peer-review process and are still a contribution to basic science, which matters greatly for your CV. But if your aim is to is affect people (i.e., change, help, or even just reach them), academic publications might not be the most direct way to do it. We pass along this professor's sentiment as an example of a successful academic who has come to appreciate other ways to think about impact.

This appreciation of impacting people's lives is the most common sentiment we have heard from PhD psychologists working outside academia. Most, if not all, of our acquaintances and professional connections have commented on the satisfaction of making a data-driven recommendation or decision that actually tangibly improves the lives of others. If you know any psychologists outside academia, you might have heard this remark as well. Examining the premise of "impact" might be one of the most rewarding parts of your journey into nonacademic jobs.

How to Adjust: Learn What Types of Impact Are Valued in Your New Workplace

In the nonacademic world, success can be measured by applying an idea and showing that it helps. This might seem simplistic in your present context, in which it can be very complicated to demonstrate that a research idea contributes unique new value to the outside world. But applying a new idea or applying it in a new way to an actual business, work, health care, or other context can really help people. The concept may be very basic or even obvious theoretically, but if no one has ever applied it or applied it correctly, you have just made a positive impact on the world. Remember reading the research article that demonstrated that handwashing prevents bacterial transmission? Neither do we, but I think we are all grateful that Ignaz Semmelweis took that idea seriously and applied it by initiating a policy that his physicians wash their hands on the way from the morgue to the labor and delivery room. Applying an idea from basic science to behaviors in the real world has undeniable merit.

Further, you have demonstrated that you are a valuable contributor to your employer. Being uniquely qualified to know about academic findings and how to apply them to make the company more efficient, please consumers more, make it easier to implement a new policy, or aid an intervention is a desirable characteristic in an employee.

> **Intervention.** An intervention is a change, experimental program, or alternative process that is carried out to improve some outcome. This term is used similarly in business settings and research settings. In a medical research setting, an intervention might be a new way for nurses to teach diabetes patients about diet. That program would be tested against current practices. In a business setting, it might be a new way for phone agents to greet customers who call.

SCIENTISTS' DIFFICULT-TO-WORK-WITH REPUTATION

In this section, we shift our perspective to discuss a premise in the nonacademic world that might affect how potential hirers perceive you.

Doctoral-level psychologists from all subfields have been working in various applied settings for many years, of course. Over that time, many of the people who work with them have developed a stereotype of academic scientists that unfortunately might be active in the places you apply to work. Certainly not everyone will hold a negative stereotype, and in settings where you are the first or only psychologist, many will be unaware of it. But you might find yourself needing to convince others, potentially even those who are interviewing you, that you do not fit that stereotype.

What is the stereotype? First, PhD scientists can be perceived as aloof, conceited, having an inflated sense of their own intelligence, and condescending. Scientists might be thought of as poor teammates, even if they are seen as earnest and friendly. Those with PhDs are often thought to be poor communicators because they are verbose or use scientific jargon or because they do not care to "come down" to communicate at the level of nonscientists. Another facet of this stereotype is that the doctorate holder will think and talk about a problem forever without actually solving it. One PhD we know who is now working outside of academia applied to corporate positions after graduating. He told us, "I received feedback from a global, publicly traded company that they would never hire someone with a PhD. The HR representative actually recommended I remove it from my résumé."

The Implication: Narrowed Career Possibilities

The effects of this stereotype are quite obvious: Demonstrating that you can break this mold can be crucial to successfully landing a career that interests you, and if this premise of others is not addressed, it can make it difficult for you to land a job or succeed in it. We do not recommend that you drop the PhD from your résumé, because if you were hired to a position that saw your degree as a liability, you would probably be quite unhappy in it. It might be helpful, though, to be aware of stereotypes that others might hold and to find ways to show that they do not fit you.

Even though this premise is not a product of your academic training, it serves as a valuable example of a mismatch between academia and other fields. The rest of the premises we examine in this book come from academia and scientific training, but it is valuable to remember that others' premises might be interfering with successful communication.

How to Adjust: Actively Foster Team-Playing Skills, Communicate Clearly, Deliver

So, how should one counter this possible premise? Simply put, practice being a good teammate. If you are up against a preconceived idea of how a scientist acts, it might be harder for you to demonstrate your team skills than for someone else. It is helpful to know this going in. Spend time listening to your teammates and learn something about them. Note areas of expertise they may have that you do not and express appreciation for that expertise. Volunteer for a few things that are not strictly part of your job. Help out when a teammate has a big project or a pressing deadline. Fair or unfair, you might have to try a little harder to show you are a good fit on the team or that you are willing and able to be a good teammate.

In a job interview, you can try to head off this premise by explaining your ability to define a problem and act on it quickly. You can refer to moments in your career when a deadline had to be met and you pulled things together quickly to deliver a quality product. A grant proposal might meet this criterion, or perhaps a last-minute institutional review board proposal that had to be written up and submitted in time to have access to that semester's participant pool. Any time you can speak directly to or frame any statements in terms of how you are decisive and prompt might be valuable.

> **Deliver.** The term *deliver* is often used instead of *turn in* or *submit* with reference to finishing an end product of a project or contract. For example, you might report to your boss, "I delivered the survey report to Jane Doe Friday afternoon."
>
> **Deliverable.** The term *deliverable* refers to the final product or tangible result of a project or contract. The deliverable could be a report, a new product, a set of recommendations, or just about anything else. Sometimes it might not yet be defined, and defining it might be one of the first steps of starting a project. This term may seem like a "buzzword," but in many business contexts it is well understood and might help set stakeholders' expectations so that no one is disappointed or upset at the final products of a project or contract.

Another way to counter this stereotype is to communicate concisely and execute. Many people are interested in discussing the psychological phenomena related to a problem; however, when a deadline is looming, or you are in a meeting in which the boss needs a conclusion, it might be time to boil things down to the bottom line, draw a conclusion, and deliver a recommendation. (We discuss communication skills at length in Chapter 5.) When you are responsible for a project or a certain deliverable, it is important to produce it on time. Assume the deadline is a hard one. Establishing a record of reliability will soon dispel any negative stereotypes about your ability to produce. One strategy that should help is to enact the old adage to "under-promise and overdeliver." If you are optimistic that you can do five things in 2 weeks, promise four things in 3 weeks. This might set you up to over-achieve, or at the very least, it will protect you against the planning fallacy. (Check out the research by Buehler, Griffin, & Peetz, 2010, on the planning fallacy if you are unfamiliar with it—it is very useful!)

WRAP-UP

In this chapter, we introduced four broad premises that will likely have general implications for any social scientist who looks for work or starts a career in a nonacademic setting. Like any of the premises in this book, they may not apply to everyone, and the implications will be different or more nuanced based on your field and the individual circumstances of your position. However, thinking through whether these premises are operating and their implications for your career search can help you proactively challenge them in preinterview steps and in the interview.

In the rest of the book, we shift focus away from defining and examining premises themselves and look toward more specific, concrete courses of action you can take to prepare for your dream career. Premises will take more of a background role as points of reference.

TAKEAWAYS

- There is considerable value in the old research findings that might not be "hot" in your field right now. Recognize that bias, and use those old classics!

- Discussing methodology in exhaustive detail might hinder your success. (Rigor is, of course, still necessary.)

- Recognize the ways to have an impact in the world—in addition to the ways that academia quantifies it.

- Professionals in other fields also have premises that might be a barrier you need to overcome—like a stereotype of how scientists work.

WHAT TO DO NOW

1. If the discussion of the third premise (impact) rang true to you, this exercise should help remind you of some other perspectives.

   The main activity in this exercise is being away from schoolwork. We recommend that you find time to go off campus and socialize with people other than the students in your program (or if you do spend time with them, do not talk about work). The hard part is to be away from work not just physically but also mentally. It can be difficult, but resist the tendency to mull over your latest idea, what that recent statistical result means, or how you will frame the introduction to the paper you are writing. The goal is to gain some perspective outside of your lab, your department, even your university. What are other ways of judging impact or success?

   One way to broaden your perspective is to talk with nonacademics, and listen. You can ask them some of these questions:

   a. In your industry, what are the most valued things you can have on your résumé?

   b. How do you show your boss that you are excelling?

   c. What does success look like at work? What does happiness or fulfillment look like outside work?

   d. Where do you find meaning?

   e. What is important to you? Professionally? Personally?

   This exercise may start to feel rather existential. The point is for you to see that there are alternative value systems out there besides what academia has built. Failure to get an article published is simply a minor professional setback. By the same token, success within academia's value system might not carry the same weight in other fields. Recognizing this can help you keep a healthy perspective on your own academic successes and challenges; when it comes to your job search, this understanding can better prepare you to discuss your qualifications with potential hirers in many other settings.

   Other professional fields have their own value systems and their own way of quantifying success. We feel, however, that the immersive nature and sheer duration of psychological science training makes it quite easy to forget that the value system is rooted in a professional field and might not be wholly generalizable elsewhere. Don't let this pattern impede your career search.

2. Consider the fourth premise we discuss in this chapter (scientists' work style). This premise is a challenge you might have to overcome when you journey into a nonacademic setting. In this exercise, we ask that you take the perspective of a nonpsychologist—someone out in the workforce who sometimes works in teams with scientists. Imagine you have, instead of PhD training, 5 or 6 years of experience in your professional field after college and you have risen a few levels in your job.

Now take a moment to consider: Which premises might have contributed to the negative stereotype of scientists?

Put another way, which behaviors coming from academic premises have influenced scientists' behaviors in the nonacademic workplace? How might these behaviors have given the impression to others that a scientist was aloof? That the scientist was not interested in being a good teammate? Choose a premise, and think about what behaviors that might support. Even if those behaviors are perfectly appropriate in the academic world, how might they be interpreted differently in a nonacademic setting? From the perspective of an established (nonscientist) professional in that field, how might those behaviors look?

PART II PACKING YOUR BAGS: IDENTIFYING YOUR SKILL SET

Now that you have thought about premises and how they might be operating, we turn to a discussion of your expertise, experiences, and abilities. We refer to these collectively as your *skills*. Before you venture out into the nonacademic workplace, it is worthwhile to examine what you want to take with you.

Postgraduate academic training has equipped you with many valuable skills. That training, however, comes with some premises that might obscure how useful or desirable your skills are outside academia. In addition, the nonacademic market also expects some skills that are not explicitly taught in scientific training. The next three chapters discuss how to take a fresh look at your skill set and how to supplement skills that might be lacking so that you will be well prepared for the journey.

3 FIVE TRANSFERABLE SKILLS YOU DEFINITELY HAVE AND HOW TO TALK ABOUT THEM

In this chapter, we list some of the basic skills that any PhD candidate has and that most candidates are accustomed to describing to other academics. These are the skills that are listed on CVs, discussed in graduate classes, and understood readily by anyone in the field. We suggest ways to talk about these skills so that people without academic or psychology training can appreciate them.

We discuss five classes of skills. Each of these classes can be broken down into several specific skills or abilities. Later in the book we provide guidance for you to do just that—examine your training and capabilities to specifically identify and define many of your skills. Here we invite you to rethink how you label your skills and take a fresh look at your skills from a perspective that is not filtered by academic premises.

Resources are already available to provide guidance on how to "translate" your academic skills into terms that recruiters or hiring managers will understand in nonacademic settings. Websites, departmental colloquia or handouts, and university career offices are all good places to look (we have selected some helpful resources and listed them in the Career Development Time Line). We encourage you to take advantage of these resources but

http://dx.doi.org/10.1037/0000170-005
The Portable PhD: Taking Your Psychology Career Beyond Academia, by P. Gallagher and A. Gallagher

also to be aware that this is only one part of the puzzle—productive conversations with prospective hirers require more than just translating your CV into a résumé. A successful transition to nonacademic employment is about your mind-set. The rest of this book provides guidance on filling in the other pieces of that mind-set puzzle.

RESEARCH

People who do not have years of training in the scientific method or the nuts-and-bolts work of conducting a laboratory or field study probably will not appreciate all that goes into research. Some might think that "research" is searching online and reading a lot of material on a topic. Some might know that scientists work in labs but might picture a place with test tubes and white coats. When you have the chance to talk about your research, be prepared to explain exactly what you can do, *without jargon*. For example, many people do not know what a psychology lab looks like. Simply explaining that labs can be rooms where volunteers come in, engage in activities such as solving problems or playing a game, and are observed for how their behaviors are different under different circumstances can shed new light on what research psychologists do.

It will also be useful to explain your research skill in terms of the value it can add to a team or organization. Simply bringing any kind of data-driven mind-set can immediately add value to many contexts. As one psychologist working outside academia told us, "I was flummoxed when I discovered that much of the planning, decision-making, and judgments of success I encountered in my workplace seemed to have no basis in systematic data collection and assessment." Some hirers will highly value your ability to measure things, collect data, and draw some conclusions or insights from them.

Other organizations will have some kind of measurement or research in place, but it might be designed by nonscientists. Your expertise in experimental methods enables you to spot pitfalls in research projects that might render findings unusable or dubious or might create data that end up not addressing the problem at hand. These aspects of your research training can easily be applied to many contexts, and the key is to describe that specific aspect of your training in terms that a potential hirer or colleague can recognize.

Of course, you should be prepared to describe your particular research specialties or strengths. Remember that even if you do not consider yourself an expert in a particular technique because you only dabbled in it, you might be the *most* expert in that skill in your new context. For example, if you have designed assessment instruments, describe that skill in plain terms and, ideally, in the language of the industry or area to which you are applying. Many employers might want a psychologist to design surveys that measure employee engagement, consumer sentiment, or user reaction to products or media. You should be able to describe your ability to measure such constructs—to zero in on the important constructs, to design instruments that assess those "soft" variables with objectivity and minimal bias, and to provide nuanced psychological insights into feelings and motivations based on the results.

In general, applying this same method of translating your skills into plain, jargon-free language and, if possible, describing the value they would add can be a great way to bridge the divide between academic and nonacademic settings.

In many fields and industries, the method for doing something is called a *process*. A fully developed process involves defining and recording all details involved, such as the steps to follow. A fully defined process could look something like a Methods section in a research report, with every detail documented. Many processes are more loosely documented or not documented or defined at all. When you interview for a nonacademic job, consider asking questions that will help you understand how various processes are taught or documented. For example, you might simply ask, "Do you follow a certain procedure to document and train employees on your processes?" If the hirer expresses the need for more rigorous process documentation, that could be an opportunity for you to add value.

Research in business settings. People use several methods for conducting research in business settings. You might come across terms such as *A/B testing*, which is comparing two variations of some process or intervention; *champion/challenger testing*, which is running a variation or new process in a small sample of the whole and comparing the results; *pilot testing*; or *process engineering*. If this is an area that you would like to pursue, it would be very useful to understand those terms, especially how they are used in the industry in which you would like to work. These terms might also be used interchangeably.

Certain practitioners have substantial experience with accepted research methods for applied settings, and many of them conduct perfectly sound research that yields usable information. Many practitioners, however, never received formal training or were trained in traditions that are not science based. That in itself does not mean they are not capable of good research or that the findings will not be valuable, and we certainly recommend treading lightly when having this discussion on the job or with potential hirers. Giving the impression that you will denigrate others' work is not a good interview strategy!

How Research Skills Add Value to an Organization

A behavioral scientist can bring high-quality behavioral research training to the table. In many contexts, your scientific training can set you apart in ways that might be hard to appreciate and articulate. Here are three ways that scientists can add unique value to an organization:

1. Some industry practitioners might not be up-to-date with the latest innovations. If you are, say so. One rule of thumb is that innovations from the academic world take several years to spread in business application; if your lab is among the leaders in a new research design or methodology, you will likely be at the forefront in the applied world. That is not to say no one will have heard of it, but widespread adoption is probably further off. You definitely have a leg up on the competition here. As part of your job search, in fact, we encourage you to discover how research is typically conducted in your new field or a related one. In an interview setting, this knowledge will not only show that you are connected to the industry but likely help you know how to communicate your ideas with potential hirers. In addition, being conversant in research innovations that made their way from the lab to the workplace in that industry might put you ahead of other candidates. In a methodology-focused role, we recommend you get to know the state of the industry you hope to enter.

2. Your training could help design a testing program or add to an existing one.

Testing program. A *testing program* is any formal or informal effort to learn new things in a company. It could take many forms, such as measuring the results of training classes or tracking the speed or accuracy of one business process over another.

Those companies that have active testing programs will likely be interested in what novel value you could add. A good independent scientist is trained to find a way to improve upon what is out there, to add a wrinkle to an existing process, or to shore up a program that has a weakness. Those skills can add value to already up-and-running research programs, which you might find in a big company with an already-established team.

3. Your training has prepared you to build a research program from the ground up. If you are vying for a position that would be responsible for creating a research program, you should highlight the "independent scientist" aspect of your training. A psychology researcher would not earn the PhD without demonstrating the ability to originate, design, and carry out research. This kind of position is more likely in a smaller company or one that is just starting up a research function.

Of course, in some contexts you will not be the only scientist, and maybe not even the only behavioral scientist. There may even be experts in product or process development who use sophisticated industry-specific methods for rapid testing and learning. In these settings you might not be the most qualified researcher—rather, your specific areas of expertise will likely be what set you apart.

Premise Example: What *Research Freedom* Means

One concern we have often heard from psychologists thinking of leaving academia is that they would lose the freedom and autonomy that academia grants. We agree that a tenured professorship sounds like a position that allows for great intellectual autonomy. But there might be other ways to think about freedom and flexibility. If you are involved in conducting tests in a business setting, the results will be used to inform decisions, not to determine your success. As one psychologist friend put it,

> I can test a theory or verify that someone's intervention is having the intended effect and not have to worry about the consequences if it doesn't reflect the desired results. I'm not worried about how it will affect grants, my ability to publish, or my chances of getting tenure. It is unbelievably freeing.

Another take on freedom concerns work–life balance: "It is good to be in an environment where how busy you are and how obsessively you are working is not a competition to prove identity and dedication within your field," said a psychologist we interviewed who works in training. Research studies might be just one part of a job outside academia—there might be several tasks and responsibilities that contribute to just keeping an organization running. The premise that certain research results are make-or-break for a project or a career success does not apply in many nonacademic contexts. Understanding this might help you better present and communicate your research skills.

Premise Example: Complex Research Designs

Here we mention an academic premise related to research design. The premise is that the degree of complexity of a design or of statistical procedures is linearly positively related to the value of the research finding. This premise is likely not explicitly endorsed or taught but is, we suspect, a natural outcome of being expected to master progressively more sophisticated techniques during graduate training. Of course, this premise is not necessarily true in either applied or academic settings. In applied settings, mounting any kind of real research project can be a massive undertaking. You may have the data for only a *t* test in many cases. We want to point out that something as simple as a *t* test might have quite a lot of impact—it could give an executive or other decision-maker insight or confidence in a conclusion that they never had before. In this instance, the simplicity of the *t*-test design might actually be quite a strength; the design, the data, and the conclusion should all be simple to describe, which makes them more digestible and memorable. As a result, you might have the chance to continue that line of research and to design and carry out further studies.

STATISTICS AND DATA ANALYSIS

You should be prepared to discuss all of your skills in general, plain-language terms that anyone can appreciate but also in specific and technical terms when you discuss them with other experts. During the interview process you will sometimes have two types of interviews for the same position: general—or standard—interviews, and technical interviews. *General interviews* are the interviews with people who hire everyone—the human resources (HR) department representative, a recruiter, or even the person who will be your boss if they do not have the scientific skills you have. In these interviews you will be best served to know how to communicate your statistics skills in plain but compelling language. *Technical interviews* will be with other people who have similar backgrounds or who do similar work to that for which you are being considered. In these interviews you should be prepared to speak of your skills and experience in the terms of your research area or specialty—in technical terms that only other experts would know.

Statistical skills are a prime example. Most people do not have advanced statistical skills and will very much appreciate it if you can translate what you can do into nonstatistical, and even nonmathematical, terms. This can be challenging. For example, describing the benefits of multilevel or nested modeling in nontechnical language might be something you have never attempted. But if you describe the rationale in operational terms—for example, by pointing out that children inside a classroom will have things in common, such as the same teacher, and that you know how to use statistical methods that can yield more accurate insights by accounting for that similarity—that style can be powerful. When you are in a technical interview, on the other hand, be precise in describing your skills to other experts. Chances are good that you have skills that the organization does not already have and they are looking to widen their capabilities. Accurately describing your skills could show them that you are in fact more of an expert than anyone else there, including the person conducting your technical interview.

LITERATURE SEARCH AND GENERATING RECOMMENDATIONS

Many people in decision-making roles regularly need people to gather, synthesize, and report information, often with concrete recommendations for how to make decisions or take action. A position that interests you might involve this kind of work.

Many people without scientific training can and regularly do perform this function in their jobs. Why would a PhD be needed to do that work? The answer is, often, that a PhD is not needed. A smart, objective person can probably review nontechnical or nonscientific materials and provide quite accurate summaries and recommendations. When the materials are technical or scientific, however, an accurate conclusion requires an expert in the area or someone who can objectively assess the quality of the materials. A CEO might want to know if increased communication with managers really has a big effect on employee engagement. Only a scientist (or, to be fair, someone with many years of on-the-job training in interpreting scientific reports, which is a rare bird) can review the academic and professional literature and weight findings by the quality of the research methods that yielded them to provide an objective answer to that CEO. Those literatures are normally the only sources of information that have empirical findings from rigorously conducted studies. In some cases, the organization interviewing you will understand this—that might be why they are looking to hire you—but in many cases you should be prepared to describe the quality of summaries and recommendations you can provide that others cannot.

One way to stand out is to be accurate in these recommendations. If a research literature has strong empirical support for a technique but the technique has never been directly tested in a work environment, you should report that, and set expectations that some testing and learning may be required to fit it properly to your workplace. If your literature includes actual tests of something in a work setting, you can carefully take some learnings from that literature and include them in your recommendation.

WRITING

If you are a published research scientist, you can clearly point to those publications as evidence of your expertise in scientific and/or technical writing. What potential employers might not understand is your ability to learn new types of writing. This skill, we believe, is underappreciated by research scientists and potentially by hirers. That you know certain types of writing is valuable; that you can learn how to effectively write in *new* styles might be even more valuable. One of our PhD psychologist friends who has worked in marketing and consulting told us she was quite surprised to find that some of the very things that were discouraged in academic writing were vital in other applications; along the same lines, Ashleigh had to learn to avoid the active voice in some policy writing (opposite what she learned in graduate school). These examples highlight the differences in writing demanded by different contexts.

We will state it again: The ability to learn new types of writing is a valuable skill. You have likely already demonstrated this skill in your training—in writing scientific research reports, in composing conference poster presentations, and especially in writing papers for scientific journals or grant proposals. Each of these is a certain type of technical writing, and you had to appeal to your audiences and compel the reader using different techniques.

This skill requires the flexibility to appreciate when a different writing style is required or preferred and the self-awareness to step back from your own thoughts and writing style to objectively assess what a project demands. If you can demonstrate or explain that you are attuned to when your writing skill might not match the audience's expectations, and that you are willing and able to learn how to modify it, you will be demonstrating that you are aware of the need to effectively communicate to nonscientists and that you will be eager to do so. This might set you apart from other academic scientists who are less aware of how premises are acting, and therefore of how nonscientists perceive them.

This readiness to learn should, of course, be extended to other communication channels besides writing. Speaking and presenting to different audiences, most of them without scientific training, can be a big part of what you do outside academia. An ability to successfully communicate science to nonscientific audiences is a great skill to include on a résumé and a valuable skill to discuss at an interview. Perhaps one of the most important qualities a potential hirer will look for is the ability to communicate to nonscientific audiences. If you do not have practice doing this, we recommend exploring some ways to practice—ideally practice that you can list on your résumé. The What to Do Now activities at the end of this chapter and in Chapter 5 of this volume provide tips on how to gain this experience.

INSIGHT INTO PEOPLE

Having insight into human nature may be so obvious that it is overlooked by many research psychologists. We have been trained to understand, more deeply than anyone, certain aspects of human thought, emotion, and behavior. Even if your focus area is narrow, you have picked up along the way a deeper knowledge of the subfields of psychology than most others have. For example, if you are a developmental psychologist who studies preschool reading development, you are still most likely more of an expert in, say, social psychology than anyone around you in a professional setting. Your first- or second-year graduate-level courses in the core subfields of psychology may seem superficial compared with the depth of your training in your specialty, but most people have never even had an upper-level undergraduate course on psychology subfields. Add that to the general knowledge you pick up during your training, the material you might teach as a teaching assistant or instructor, and the research talks you see at your department colloquia, and you are relatively expert in most of psychology. In other words, you have a well-rounded science-based appreciation of general human nature.

One aspect of this expertise that might be attractive to hirers is originality. Executives and decision-makers need insights and often look for insights that their competitors do not have.

> **Insights,** in a business context, are any novel ideas or observations that can be turned into something useful—anything from an innovative new feature for a product to a way to improve a management practice to a message that will resonate with customers. For example, showing that consumers are demonstrating the recency bias in rating the service quality of multiple interactions with a company might be a new insight. Insights can come from analyzing data (as in "big data analytics") or from applying a new idea to an established process.

There are many well-established methods of generating insights, but a psychological scientist's ideas can break away from those industry-standard practices and be truly unique. The established methods have a conventional set of variables that are assumed to be predictive of important behaviors (e.g., buying, high employee productivity). A psychologist can bring brand-new ideas to that variable set—we have 140 or so years of findings to draw from, many of which are applicable to real-world problems! Even older psychology research findings might not have been applied in some settings and can help create, for example, original products or new ways to manage teams (so a brand-new unreplicated finding is not necessary for a novel insight in many cases).

WRAP-UP

In this chapter, we briefly discussed five classes of skills that the typical PhD probably has when they finish their graduate training. Remember that the skills you have gained in your training that you might not even think to articulate could be the ones that are most compelling to hirers or in certain fields. That said, we believe that even the most accessible and compelling language that you can find to describe these basic skills can fall short of landing you a great job, or even getting your résumé and cover letter through initial stages of screening. Research psychologists should have a thorough understanding of the field(s) they want to work in, and how they write and talk about their skills should be adapted to that field. The rest of the book gives you guidance on how to explore various fields and adapt the way you present yourself accordingly.

TAKEAWAYS

- Your research skills can be defined and communicated in ways that are different from how you think of them in academia—ways that are compelling to potential hirers.

- Basic skills like literature searching and statistics skills are probably better described in nonacademic terms, ideally in terms of the value they would add.

- You have more than the ability to write for academic outlets—you have the ability to learn new ways of writing to suit a new audience.

- Deep, empirically based, original insight into people's thoughts, feelings, and behaviors is an underappreciated skill of psychologists.

WHAT TO DO NOW

1. Build a résumé.

Peruse any resources you have come across for building a résumé. Find a few that seem most helpful and follow their guidance. You can even use templates that you find online or in Microsoft Word. The Career Development Time Line lists some sources that we have found useful.

It is not crucial that you find the perfect template or figure out which of the many writers who claim they have the secret to the perfect résumé is correct. Your résumé will develop and change over time, and you will likely adapt it to several areas, so you might have three or more versions at any time. What makes the "perfect" résumé depends on the specific position to which you are applying, the industry norms or trends at the time, the hiring manager, and the screening steps you might need to pass through in the submission process; in short, there is no single perfect résumé format. You should consider all the advice you come across, weight the more credible sources more heavily, and find what works best for you through trial and error. For this particular exercise, the goal is simply to build your first draft and, while doing it, start practicing all the ways you can list your skills and accomplishments.

In our experience, students who are used to thinking of their work within the CV framework have a great deal of difficulty with several aspects of résumé writing. First is the Objective statement that is standard or expected in résumés geared toward certain job types. To many researchers, this can feel slick or disingenuous. Understanding what the Objective statement intends to communicate to the reader is vital for composing a good one. (Several resources for approaching the Objective statement are listed in the Career Development Time Line.) Second, students typically have difficulty letting go of every poster title or talk title. In a résumé, you should be able to reframe those items into skills and abilities instead of featuring each individual entry. It helps to consider the different goals and audiences of the two documents and how you can reconstrue the same information to accomplish both tasks successfully. If you have already drafted a résumé, we encourage you to take a fresh look at it for this activity.

Next, request some feedback. We recommend taking advantage of the resources at your school, such as the career office. The staff members might not regularly work with graduate students, but we suggest you ask them for advice anyway. If you explain that you are considering applying to nonacademic positions and that they can treat your résumé just as they do those of undergraduates, they might be willing to help. If you do not have access to such career resources through your school, we suggest you find feedback from someone who has held several professional positions (and has therefore spent significant time crafting their résumé) or someone who has been involved in hiring people.

Keep in mind that this is just the first step in building your résumé and all the things it summarizes—your personal brand, your value proposition(s), your skills and accomplishments. For now, we want you to experience the process of thinking through an entire draft and be mindful of each component involved in crafting it.

Personal brand and value proposition. Your *personal brand* is the sum total of your skills and abilities, your value propositions, and what makes you unique. (Part III focuses on developing the components of your personal brand.) Just as well-established consumer brands become familiar and capture and convey what the products or companies offer, a personal brand does so for you. Your value proposition is something useful that you bring to the table, stated in a way that conveys why it is valuable (more detail on value propositions is provided in Chapter 7, this volume).

2. Build a list of, and practice new ways of describing, your skills.

You can start with the skills as you listed them on your résumé, but we recommend you create a new document to keep and refer to that simply lists your skills. This document can be valuable when you start to apply for many different jobs. In it, you can build categories of skills for each industry or field you are pursuing—for example, you can have a section for your research skills, your writing skills, your marketing skills, and so on. You can also divide the list into different ways to describe the same skills—for example, the talking points about your research skills will likely be different for an HR position than for a marketing position.

Talking points. *Talking points* are brief, memorizable messages that capture the essence and nuance of a topic. They should be powerful and adaptable to your audience, and you should practice using and refining them.

The main goals of this activity are to build your first draft of this document and to start practicing. You can spend much more time perfecting this list during your career search, as you can your résumé, but a complete draft is the first step.

4

OTHER TRANSFERABLE SKILLS YOU PROBABLY HAVE AND HOW TO TALK ABOUT THEM

What is your favorite moment as a researcher? Can you remember when you had that first really sophisticated research design idea? Or maybe when you finally worked out how to test a particularly weighty hypothesis? For me (Patrick), it was when I figured out how to add a wrinkle to my dissertation research that would bring together two research areas—traits and self-control—to test a new hypothesis (see Gallagher, Fleeson, & Hoyle, 2011). For me (Ashleigh), it was the turning point of my prelim, which is an exam paper preliminary to the dissertation in which graduate students must contribute theoretical development to a research topic with minimal input from the faculty advisor.

You might never have thought about describing it this way, but the skill you probably demonstrated at that moment was *innovation*. Innovation is an ability that many companies highly value, seek in job candidates, and actively try to cultivate in their workforce—and it is a transferable skill. It is something you should certainly feature as part of your set of skills.

When operating under the premises we listed in Chapter 1, it might not occur to you to scrutinize and articulate your skills in this way. On the academic job market, those who would be evaluating your CV would easily

http://dx.doi.org/10.1037/0000170-006
The Portable PhD: Taking Your Psychology Career Beyond Academia, by P. Gallagher and A. Gallagher

recognize your innovation skills—they would simply look at your publication list and read your papers. Your ability to innovate would be inferred from this information, even if your CV readers did not describe it as such. To publish articles, and even to complete a successful dissertation, you have to figure out how to contribute something new and valuable to your field. Publications, especially high-impact ones, presuppose the ability to innovate and provide a metric for evaluating your innovation ability in the academic context.

Outside academia, many people do not recognize that innovation is a core skill of an independent scientist. Psychology researchers have other skills that fit this same profile; they are skills you might have never articulated, or might have assumed that others would already know you have, but are not obvious to nonacademics. For example, one master's level research psychologist we know discovered that outside academia, her teaching experience served as evidence that she could speak in public and organize and prepare materials to train adult learners. "None of these are skills that I would have immediately thought would be helpful in shaping a nonacademic career, but I received very positive feedback about my teaching experience when interviewing for my current job" (designing e-learning content).

In many cases your "hidden" skills will be very valuable to a hiring manager or recruiter. They might miss that you have them unless you properly communicate them.

In the following pages, we describe some soft skills that most PhDs have but might not have thought to articulate. To examine how you have demonstrated them, and to uncover other obscured skills, we recommend thinking about the professional "tricks of the trade" that you and other researchers have mastered. These are skills that professionals in any field learn that help them succeed; they are not necessarily taught in courses but rather are gleaned along the way or passed down informally from mentors to mentees. The goal is to find a way to identify, define, and describe them.

INNOVATION

Meeting doctoral program requirements, developing a program of research, and especially publishing scientific papers require the ability to analyze a current state and come up with something new that adds value. Think of what happens when you contribute to a research literature: You must assess the current status quo (i.e., a set of findings or a theory) and think about how it can be advanced, improved, or a problem resolved. You must come up with a novel proposal for how to go about it (i.e., your hypothesis or set of hypotheses). Then you must come up with a way to try it out, most likely a way that has never been tried before, and do it in a manner that yields usable intelligence about what happened and what to do next (i.e., research design, data collection and analysis).

When a recruiter or job interviewer asks you about your innovation skills, you might explain your skills in a way that the previous paragraph exemplifies. Employers are often looking for people who can be creative in thinking of new ways to do something and then plan how to test whether it works. That is, simply put, what scientific investigation often is. Any success you have had in designing and executing a research study that tested a new hypothesis is a demonstration that you have the valuable skill of innovation.

> **Test.** The term *test* is generally interchangeable with how academics use *study*. We conduct studies to test hypotheses. In an applied setting, a manager might want to try a new process or tool. She might ask you to do a test of this new process, which would mean to design a study and measure whether it outperforms the current process.

HEDGING YOUR BETS

When you design a research study, do you limit your study to a single hypothesis? Collect only one type of data? We would guess not—instead, you have several secondary hypotheses your data can speak to, and several sources of data you can capture. And you probably ensure that you have not just one dependent variable but several, so you have several opportunities to find effects. Of course, the primary hypothesis and dependent variable might be the only one that would be worthy of publication as a primary finding, but your advisor probably cautioned you against running a study that had one and only one chance of yielding informative data.

This skill of casting a broad-enough net would likely be obvious to academic job search committees through conversations with your references or reading your publications. At least, if it was not apparent from your publications, another researcher would know to ask you about it if they desired. Outside of academia, a hiring manager or recruiter might not even know to ask. Ultimately, this may or may not be a skill that finds its way onto your résumé, but if not, we recommend you find a way to feature it in interviews. Executives and managers are always interested in someone with the ability to maximize their investments—in this case, a proposed research project might be a cost that many managers would look for any reason to deny. When you can describe how you will generate useful intelligence no matter what the results reveal, you will likely win support for your work. Describing that skill in the right terms could be valuable.

PROJECT MANAGEMENT

A master's thesis and a doctoral dissertation are major long-term projects. They required you to successfully navigate at least some of a long list of challenges: gathering resources, designing new systems or tools, lining up funding, managing people, anticipating potential problems, adapting quickly when problems arise, learning from mistakes, managing time deadlines, and ultimately delivering a tangible product. You can describe each of those skills in detail (and you should be prepared to), but taken together you can also talk about them as your expertise in project management.

It may come as a surprise to you, but many companies have entire teams of people whose job is to manage projects—not their own projects, but others'. Indeed, in many cases it makes economic sense to hire people to ensure the smooth execution of major projects, which in some organizations results in a Project Management Office. Most psychology PhDs can accurately claim to have quite a bit of experience managing projects. Do not hesitate to mention your project management skills, and even list them on a résumé. Examine what you did, in detail, in planning and then managing the many challenges and speed bumps that came up while carrying out your biggest research projects. Practice describing what you did, and what you learned, in jargon-free ways.

It is important to note here that the term *project management* has a specific definition that will likely be familiar to many interviewers. As we mentioned, it is an actual position and/or career—you can receive formal training and certification in it. Be aware that when you use this term, you might need to explain that you do not have training in any formal discipline of project management but rather that you are speaking generally about your skills in organizing and directing major projects. If it does appear on your résumé, you might find yourself fielding inquiries from recruiters looking for career project managers.

If you are interested in the idea of formal systems of project management, your career development center or graduate school might offer professional development courses in it. Community colleges usually offer brief workshops on project management that can orient you to this profession. You can also find resources online that might be worth reading through to familiarize yourself with the discipline and terminology—it would not hurt in a professional context to know a bit about this.

BUILDING COALITIONS

As a professional academic researcher, publishing research and obtaining grants are crucial. To be successful in those areas, other people must critically review your work and approve it or sign off on it. There are several ways to improve the chances of that approval at which most successful researchers are very skilled. As it turns out, these skills are valuable outside academia as well.

One such skill is building coalitions. These coalitions can be formal and explicit, such as societies dedicated to specific research areas, or smaller informal groups of people who have common interests. If you are a member of such a group, you are likely to enjoy several benefits, and friendly reviews are at the top of the list. Let's say a savvy scientist has identified others who are sympathetic to the ideas or findings they are presenting. Even better, that scientist knows others for whom it is strategically advantageous to publish their work. Knowing, through whatever channels are available, on which grant review boards or journals those friendly reviewers are currently serving can be crucial for sustaining a string of publications or grants. It is in researchers' best interests to build, and contribute to, these networks. Ideally, good research would be published solely on its own merit, but there is empirical evidence that affiliations matter (e.g., Tomkins, Zhang, & Heavlin, 2017).

Finding a "champion," a person who is willing to promote you or your work to others, is one specific way of building coalitions that many academics master. When in the running for an academic position, it is advantageous to have a champion on the inside—a respected voice who promotes you to hirers. Remember we use the term *hirers* as shorthand for anyone who might interview you to pay you for your services, such as a hiring manager, a consulting client prospect, or an investor. A reviewer who can endorse you or your work to an editorial decision-maker can also be a powerful asset in publishing your work.

Recognizing when a champion would be beneficial and cultivating relationships that result in champions can apply to almost any workplace. Ideas and proposals are debated daily in most business settings, and the ability to make yours succeed can advance your career and might impress a hirer. Think about how to articulate this skill, and watch for opportunities to mention it in interviews, writings, proposals, or cover letters.

Identifying a network of people who are motivated to see your work succeed can also be a useful skill to develop. Scientists whose work is top quality may never establish a track record of publishing and funding because they do not establish such a network. Similarly, many professionals with brilliant ideas that can really help organizations never find the career they are after because they do not identify the people to whom it is advantageous that they succeed (or that their ideas succeed).

Such strategic analysis is sometimes not necessary. The merit of your ideas might be all that is needed to ensure your success. In some organizations, managers might be attuned to employees' ideas enough that good ideas are heard no matter who has them and how they present them.

But just as it is in academia, outside of academia there could be 200 other people who can contribute quality work just as you can. Cultivating a coalition is a good way to set yourself apart. Your practice of this skill inside the academic world can be applied directly to contexts outside of it. And if you can appropriately make a hirer aware of this skill, you might stand out among other candidates. We recommend that you practice describing this trick of the trade in ways that general audiences will understand. We also recommend that you tailor the way you describe it to the career you are targeting—for example, in sales-related roles it might be fine to be explicit about this skill, but in a research and development role you might highlight it differently. "Building coalitions" might be a good label for it and might even be appropriate for a résumé. The ability to build relationships with others and win champions for your work—people who will put their support behind it when others review it—is another way to describe this skill.

We also recommend describing this skill in terms of a team's ideas instead of your own. If you are applying for a role on a team whose ideas or proposals you will be presenting or promoting, this skill is one that a hirer will probably like to hear. Again, if you act according to the premises found in an academic setting in which most players will know to evaluate your expertise in this skill, you might never communicate this important skill to hirers. Outside of academia, most people have no idea that this kind of coalition building is part of the scientific landscape. It is up to you to bring it into the conversation in a hiring situation.

Building coalitions is a good example of what might be considered a soft skill. *Soft skills*, which are also the subject of a formal research literature in which they are called "employability skills," are your abilities that you might not list on your résumé but will still increase your chances of getting and succeeding in a job. Of course, if you are applying for a leadership position or a consulting position in which you would lead team-building workshops, listing this skill would be appropriate. For other positions, however, it might be something that comes up in an interview that you can speak to as a general competency. In still other contexts, it might simply be something you can use in a new position to build strong ties to your new teams or supervisor(s).

> **Competency.** *Competencies* are a broader way to describe skills, experience, and abilities. You might find job listings that require certain competencies. For example, leadership might be listed as a competency. Leadership might include specific skills like coalition building, experience in leadership positions, a natural ability to connect with people, and knowledge learned from a leadership training course. In this book we use the terms *skills* and *knowledge*, and you can refer to the résumé-building sources we provide in the Career Development Time Line to appropriately describe your qualifications for different contexts.

STRATEGIC FRAMING

Strategic framing is another way to increase the probability of a favorable review of your work. When a researcher writes a scientific paper, the introduction places the research into a context of other findings, theoretical traditions, and perhaps potential applications. A single finding might be placed in one of several "camps" or research streams. For example, when writing up Patrick's dissertation research, we would have written slightly different Introduction and Discussion sections if we had decided to submit to a personality-centered journal over a journal that published all types of social and personality research.

Framing your work to maximize its chances of favorable evaluation is a skill that can be valuable in applied settings. If you are an employee in an organization, the work that can propel you or your team upward in your career might need to be proposed and approved. If you are working as an independent consultant, you will need approval on engagement proposals or specific project proposals from clients. The ability to fit those proposals into the interests of your reviewers can be powerful.

DISCOVERING YOUR SOFT SKILLS

This chapter lists broad examples of transferable skills and how you might reconceptualize them for a job search outside academia. How else might you discover and practice describing such skills?

Fortunately, many existing communities and resources can help. One source can be business plans. Learning about business plans can help you become familiar with the kinds of issues that concern many businesses and even nonprofits. It will give you an appreciation of what many hirers or people in other roles have to do and think about in their day-to-day work. In many settings it will be highly advantageous if you can think in those terms and speak of your skills accordingly. Understanding your boss's or clients' concerns is a crucial skill in delivering high-quality, satisfying work products. Knowing the purposes and contents of business plans is a great way to start learning these ideas.

A second source for discovering transferable skills is local business, entrepreneurship, or coworking communities. Several of these groups are mainly concerned with helping small businesses start up or succeed. These communities might be helpful to you because you will likely find people there who are open-minded, comfortable with adapting on the fly, and accustomed to creatively exploring how new people can help one another succeed. The entrepreneurial community is often willing to listen to new and different ideas and to change direction quickly. They are also often on the lookout for new and unique talent. Familiarizing yourself with their world and participating in it can give you brand-new ways of assessing your talents and skills, as well as suggest new ways of describing them. A bonus benefit of participating in these communities is that they can reveal emerging business opportunities or trends that can give you clues about where to look for jobs.

A third source for discovering soft skills is employability studies or skills inventories provided by professional associations, government or college offices, or commercial organizations (e.g., Minnesota State CAREERwise, 2012; National Association of Colleges and Employers, n.d.; Society for Human Resource Management, 2016). These sources conduct research and provide advice on the types of skills employers look for. As you assess your experiences and training, referencing these sources can prompt you to look for different skills or to reconsider how to label the ones you already feature. In general, research literature and other resources on employability skills (sometimes also called "job readiness" skills) can give you an idea of general capabilities that employers look for. Of course, every job requires a different mix of skills, but many hirers expect a certain level of basic professional and/or social ability.

WRAP-UP

Many of the skills you have developed as a graduate student or a postdoc might be considered basic social or political skills that can be useful in any line of work. We think, however, that some of them—like the ones discussed in this chapter—may be specifically sought after by hirers, and may be especially hard for you to recognize.

We encourage you to continuously analyze what you do to look for hidden skills and think about and practice how to articulate them. We also suggest that as you explore the nonacademic landscape, you keep an eye out for what hirers in your chosen industries are looking for in candidates. Find the skills they ask for, and if you come across career-specific jargon or ill-defined skills or constructs, dig around until you find the core skills they seek. Then take a fresh look at what your training has built in you. Is there overlap? What do you have that they need?

TAKEAWAYS

- The premises that underlie academic standards, methods, and tricks of the trade can obscure valuable transferable skills.

- Innovation, hedging your bets to ensure success, project management, coalition building, and strategic framing are five examples of skills that most psychologists should have and might be hidden.

- Analyze what you do in terms of what hirers look for to identify your hidden or implicit skills.

WHAT TO DO NOW

1. Learn about business plans.

    Find some sample business plans, or plans for businesses that have been successful. Acquaint yourself with their main components and what belongs in each section. All this can be done easily by searching online.

You will find many, many examples, and soon you will start to recognize common themes and what it takes to have good material for each section. You should also start recognizing those that are more blustery and buzzwordy as opposed to substantive and powerfully written.

You can learn about business in general from perusing business plans from a variety of industries. If, however, there are a few industries or fields you are interested in, gather plans from those industries.

If you have the time and interest, you can take one of the courses offered by many organizations to learn how to build business plans. Your university's graduate school or career center likely has some material. Local chambers of commerce or small business groups might have some training.

Studying business plans is a great way to learn about the skills that nonacademic hirers are looking for. The plans that you find should guide you in examining what you do and give you ideas for uncovering obscured skills in your toolbox. Match what you do to what is needed to carry out business plans. Practice describing your skills in ways that appeal to writers and consumers of business plans.

You may never need to write or read a business plan. However, this exercise can be valuable because it can help you recognize skills you might not understand are transferable and because it can give you clues about how to communicate to potential hirers. Of course, if you ever entertain the notion of starting your own business, be prepared to have to sell someone on your ideas in a format like this. If someone is going to invest in you, loan you money, or otherwise support or join you, you will need to demonstrate that you have concrete and comprehensive plans for sustaining revenue and profitability. And even if you never find yourself in the position to propose a full business plan, your preparation will make you more conversant in explaining how your skills can add value in many contexts, and generally communicate to people in compelling ways.

A couple notes to remember:

- A business plan is often used to convince people to invest in a venture or new business, and you might not be interested in that. In that case, focus just on understanding why others need to know the information that business plans contain.

- If you are applying for a job at a big or established company, business plan material is likely not applicable. You and the teams who interview you might never need to work directly on business plan materials. We believe it is still a good exercise for academics to practice when preparing for a nonacademic career.

2. Make connections with professionals outside of academia.

    For the purpose of finding obscured skills, venturing out and talking to people can be a valuable way to gain new perspectives on what you do.

    You can contact others in several ways, and here are some to start exploring:

- Your local chamber of commerce: Contact someone to ask what social groups they host, sponsor, or list for job seekers—or better, for those seekers who are looking to transition careers.
- Meetup groups of job seekers or entrepreneurs: Explore groups and meet people to start building a network.
- Coworking spaces: Some host social events for nonmembers or offer affordable memberships.
- Local startup incubators
- Your local Small Business Development Center (SBDC) office
- Service Corps of Retired Executives mentoring (https://www.score.org).

Once again, we recommend that you be open and honest about your career status and what you are looking to work on. Ask others what they think of what you do and what is valuable in their industry.

We also recommend that you do not treat this experience as a course for which you show up and simply soak up others' guidance. These are communities, and you will find you are much more welcome if you are willing to contribute to others' success as well as benefit from others' help. Be prepared to volunteer some time, to put in a few hours here and there helping someone else with their challenges, or to listen and give feedback to others' ideas. The more value you contribute, the more you will reap. And of course, another benefit of being a member of a community is finding otherwise hidden career opportunities.

5

SKILLS YOU MAY NEED TO ACQUIRE OR REFINE

In the previous two chapters, we discussed skills for which you have been trained. Chapter 3 in this volume featured skills that you, and pretty much anyone else, know that PhDs have. In Chapter 4, we discussed some skills that your PhD training equips you with but that you might not think to mention in a nonacademic setting.

In this chapter, we turn our attention to skill sets that are valuable in your transition from academia to other fields but for which you may not have been trained. A social psychologist we know who has built his own management consultant practice told us, "My clients value me being able to understand a variety of things that were not covered in grad school for psychology—understanding finance and reading financial statements, helping with strategy, key performance indicators, and knowing the terminology of business." This sentiment illustrates the idea that your success outside academia might depend on developing skills that are not typically addressed in graduate school curricula.

These skills may not be specific to any industry or field—rather, they are skills that will help just about anyone land, and be successful in, different positions. They can also be particularly important for academically trained

http://dx.doi.org/10.1037/0000170-007
The Portable PhD: Taking Your Psychology Career Beyond Academia, by P. Gallagher and A. Gallagher

job seekers because they will help you have high-quality, effective communication with colleagues, network connections, and potential hirers. Three of the four skill classes we discuss in this chapter are styles of communication. The fourth set of skills—teamwork—is closely related to communication. Considering the premise mismatches that many academics will face with potential hirers and the barriers to communications they will present, the skills in this chapter are important to practice.

SIMPLICITY AND BREVITY

As a graduate student, you might be apprehensive about simplifying. If you simplify something too much, it might appear as though you don't understand it thoroughly. For example, if you are giving a talk and need to summarize a long or complex line of research to lead up to your hypotheses, you have to be very careful to give all the requisite details to justify your hypotheses and set up your findings and conclusions. If you do not, you can expect some questions from the audience about those details! Generally, the graduate school experience is not set up to reward your simplifying material.

Along with the fear that simplifying too much will show that you don't know your stuff, there is also a premise at work here that we listed in Chapter 1: There is resistance from academia to doing too much "selling." It can be seen as disingenuous or in bad taste to rely on anything other than the details of the actual methods and findings to promote research. It can even be seen as "selling out."

We believe the picture can be more nuanced than that. We certainly agree that overstating findings, overgeneralizing findings, or taking too many logical leaps in claims about how research can be applied is inappropriate and bad for our science. Simplifying how you communicate about research, however, is not the same as those actions. It takes considerable skill and practice to faithfully convey the core findings of research in a way that anyone can understand, without losing the novelty and power, and that does not necessarily diminish the quality of the research or reflect badly on the field.

Certain scientists are skilled at simplifying. You have probably come across some of them in research reports, conference talks, popular publications, or personal communications. We invite you to reflect a bit about how you feel when you attend one of those talks or read one of those reports. As for us, we feel thankful! It is refreshing and enjoyable to listen to a research talk that is clear and easy to process. Indeed, fluency research supports the idea that information that is easy to perceive and/or process is experienced as more pleasant (Oppenheimer, 2008). You can exert greater mental effort on the big ideas and findings and less effort finding your way through the weeds of technical jargon and microscopic methodology details. Of course, if the subject matter is central to your work, you may later scrutinize the key details of the research before you pass your final judgment on the merits and importance of the findings. But the scientist has made a compelling initial case that they have uncovered something new and valuable.

When Might You Need to Simplify Research Findings?

You might be wondering when you will need to simplify and communicate research to nonscientists. It certainly depends on the position you take or the situation, but here are several possibilities:

- **A job interview.** You might be directly asked to describe not only your research, which you should be able to communicate simply, but also the line of research on which it was built and how your contribution advanced theory. Although it is perfectly apparent to you (and your advisor and dissertation committee, for that matter) why your research was valuable, it might be a mystery to your interviewer. It is vital in that situation to demonstrate that you can convey the details and the meaning of research in an accessible and compelling way.

- **Professional presentations or consulting engagements.** When you are delivering a presentation or proposal, you will sometimes need to cite research that supports your assertion or idea—indeed, in many positions you will be expected to base your proposals or recommendations on empirical evidence. You should have practice summarizing the research that supports your material, whether it's your own research or others', and explaining concisely and convincingly why it supports your proposal. This might even be relevant on your own team. If your boss and teammates are not scientists and you are building something to present to an executive as a team, you might need to support a position you advocate by explaining research findings to them.

- **Informal professional conversations.** Meeting people with whom you work or colleagues from other organizations are great opportunities to build your professional network, gain support in a job, or learn about possible job leads. Having concise, impactful insight from your science that will fascinate people and that they will remember (and ideally that applies to their work or life) will generally make a good impression.

Of course, a pontificating professor who knows more than you about everything is not a fun party conversationalist; but if you clearly know your science and speak compellingly about it, you are more likely to make people interested in thinking about you for open positions.

The Challenge of Simplicity

Think about a favorite research paper you have read recently—one with a result you found really intriguing or profound. Could you "dumb it down"? Probably—summarizing something in a sentence or two is generally pretty easy. Simplifying while retaining the full impact, however, takes more skill and practice. Could you explain the novelty of the new finding to a friend or family member (not a scientist) and get them as excited about it as you were? That would probably be more challenging.

Just dumbing down research can bleach it of its impact. That is how valuable basic science can be perceived as merely common sense. For example, describing cognitive dissonance reduction as simply "making yourself feel better" can make it seem like a trivial contribution and lead people to question why an organization might invest in research on such a topic. Describing it, however, as shown in the following passage probably makes it easier for the listener or reader to appreciate how it can have quite a profound impact on people's lives or work:

> Cognitive dissonance is discomfort that a person feels when they hold two or more contradictory beliefs, ideas, or values. People can do surprising things to reduce that discomfort, including changing or adjusting long-held values or beliefs.

It will serve you well to think of a straightforward way that a finding can impact your audience's daily lives or major decisions and include that concisely when you present a finding. These real-life connections can make a finding quite compelling. Of course, many people are fascinated by psychology research simply for the insights it provides into being human. But in a professional presentation or interview context, your audience might need something other than inherent interest to approve a proposal or decide to hire you.

When the power of a finding is in the main effect or the simple bivariate relationship, communicating the point is relatively easy. For example, there is evidence that introverts find social interactions taxing, and so building a workplace that allows people to self-select into very public or more private areas might increase productivity. When the power of a finding is in the nuance, it is harder to convey that nuance in a way that an audience might find easy to understand. As an example, consider the following passage from *The Secret Life of Pronouns* by James Pennebaker (2011). Pennebaker wrote of gleaning information about psychological constructs from language style,

> People who are analytical thinkers tend to use articles, prepositions, and negations when describing a boring bottle, a backyard party, or talking with their neighbor about Mrs. Gilliwitty's stomach problems. Of course, the ways we talk and think change depending on the situations we are in. In formal settings, we all talk more formally; at wild parties, we are apt to talk, well, more wildly. Nevertheless, we take our personalities with us wherever we go. (pp. 98–99)

You have probably already recognized how a premise is at work here. If your scientific training has resulted in the perception of a positive linear relationship between complexity in research and statistics, on one hand, and the impact or value of research findings, on the other, that would be a strong disincentive to simplify how you talk about research. Relatedly, and as discussed in Chapter 4 of this volume, in many contexts in academia you are expected to defend the details of your design or rationale (and no detail is too small to affect results!). Your default habit, understandably, might have become the recitation of those details. That habit works against simple, clear communication between you and those outside academia.

The Challenge of Brevity

Have you written a journal article with a 2,500-word limit? Perhaps 1,500 words? It's a challenge to squeeze all that information in, right? In many nonacademic communications, 1,500 words will be a luxury. So far, we have discussed only simplicity, but here we discuss its close cousin, brevity.

Obviously, the two often go hand in hand. For example, if you sum up a research article in a few simple sentences, not only have you simplified it (we hope) but it is much briefer. But it might not be brief enough—you might be given only a few bullet points on one PowerPoint slide or just a few seconds during a presentation or meeting to introduce and explain a research finding. Routinely I (Patrick) find myself in a meeting with an executive or leadership team and am asked a question that I cannot answer without explaining a bit of research. If I take too much time to set up the research, explain the finding, and then connect it to the problem at hand, people become bored and distracted or, worse, start to discount the value of having me there. The more quickly I can describe the key value of the research to the problem at hand, the more value I can bring. If someone would like more detail on the research, then I can say more, or invite the person to talk after the meeting.

Luckily, our academic training includes some preparation for this skill in the form of writing abstracts. Boiling down the essential components of a paper into 150- or 250-word summaries is good practice for being brief. When writing an abstract for an article, the goal is generally to be comprehensive and accurate—to cover the information a reader expects and needs to see to judge the potential utility of the article. When writing an abstract as a proposal or submission, perhaps for a conference presentation, another goal is to be compelling. In both cases, density is normally not a bad thing; in fact, high density—a lot of information crammed into every sentence—is probably the best strategy for achieving the purposes of the abstract. In non-academic communications, there is often not a set format or expectations, so you need to decide which information is best to present first. It might be the bottom-line finding, or it might be how a finding can help solve someone's problem. Here, density will work against you. Brevity will not mean much if the message is so dense that someone needs to hear or read it multiple times to extract all the information. Being brief requires being adaptable and learning what works in which situations.

When discussing research in a context in which simplicity and brevity are needed, it is acceptable to exclude details you would share in an academic context. This certainly does not mean you can be inaccurate; every summary or description you give should be accurate. It just does not have to include all the methodology details and caveats you might focus on in, say, a graduate seminar. For example, imagine you are presenting the results of an employee survey to an executive leadership team, and an executive asks you why the results of some recent employee focus groups are more favorable than the results of your survey. You might reply, "A research area called 'group dynamics' has identified several processes that often unfold in small-group settings that can cause the group's conclusions to be different from what any individual member feels or thinks." That statement is accurate—it does not include methodology, moderators, or even a description of specific effects—but it is accurate. Your audience might ask you to elaborate then and there, and you can go into more detail about specific findings, such as group polarization or risky shift. Alternatively, there might not be time, and you might be asked, for example, to write up some recommendations for how and when to use focus groups versus surveys. The initial, brief summary of the results, which should catch attention and be obviously pertinent to the current discussion, will allow the audience or client to either ask for more or simply trust your expertise and move on.

The ability to quickly summarize relevant research findings does not come easy, especially after training for years in an environment where detail and lengthy exposition is the norm (and indeed often required). It takes practice, thoughtful composition, and adaptability. You will describe some results often enough that you will come to have brief summarizations of them at the ready, and other results you will have to summarize on the fly. Both skills are good to build.

In some cases, brevity is an absolute must. You may have something like 10 minutes and four slides to present your ask. In informal professional discussions, it will often serve you well to be quick (but of course compelling) about your science so as not to bog down what the other person(s) intended to be a quick exchange. In other cases, you might have more time to do a presentation—perhaps in an internal meeting. In those cases, you might want to unfold a story or two that helps people appreciate the implications of some research.

> **Ask (n).** A request, for example of someone's time, funds, or approval. If you write or call someone and spend a lot of time setting up your request, they might say, "So, what's the ask?"–they want you to define what it is you are requesting from them. It is similar to what is called the "call to action" in marketing. Coming to the point quickly and defining it clearly usually results in faster and better responses.

For your professional development, we highly recommend the book *Made to Stick* by Chip and Dan Heath (2007). Their book is all about effective communication, includes guidance for practicing simplicity and brevity. Studying the skill of effective communication is a relatively cheap investment that can pay off immensely no matter what career you pursue. If you are brave enough, we recommend that you try leaving out the details and being simple and brief sometime at school, maybe in your next class meeting. See if anyone seems thankful!

BROADCASTING YOUR SCIENCE

Earlier we talked about simplifying and summarizing research findings for targeted purposes. In this section, we discuss more general issues of communication—persuading someone of the value of your science or why a PhD is preferable for the role for which you are applying. This could take the form of an hour-long guest presentation, a conversation with an interviewer for a job, or an ongoing conversation that happens when you pass a teammate or executive in the hall once in a while. This section might also be called "Promoting Your Science" or "Teaching Your Science."

Fortunately, there is an ever-growing library of examples of psychology research described in nonscientific terms; we list some of them next. Most of the examples we list are in the areas of social psychology and the related subfield of behavioral economics, perhaps because the research often lends itself to satisfy people's natural interest in social interactions or because it is easy to describe why many of the findings can be relevant to personal or professional issues.

Recommended Popular Science Books

Some of these popular science books are written by the psychologists themselves, and others are written by science writers or authors. Some are considered nonscientific but denser and/or less explicit about how the research can be or has been applied to real-world problems. Some have made an impact in the business world—companies or individuals have used them as guides to applying behavioral science in their company or individual role. An endless stream of books is aimed at helping professionals achieve more, be more efficient and productive, or be more effective leaders. Most of the books are not science based (whether they claim to be or not), but the ones listed next are. As a scientist, one of the abilities you bring to a company or client is that you can tell the difference. (Full publication details of these books are provided in the reference list.)

- Books that are making an impact in the business/public/policy world: *Nudge*; *The Last Mile*; *The Power of Habit*; *Thinking, Fast and Slow*; *Predictably Irrational* (and other Dan Ariely books); *The Happiness Advantage*; *The Best Place to Work*; *Broadcasting Happiness*; *Drive*; *Stumbling on Happiness*; *The Power Paradox*; *Mindset*; *The Paradox of Choice*; *Flow*; *The Narcissism Epidemic*; *Generation Me*; *Quiet*; *Influence*; *Flourish*

- Books written by scholars highly esteemed in their field: *The Curse of the Self*; *Clash! How to Thrive in a Multicultural World*; *The Righteous Mind*; *Why We Do What We Do*; *Redirect*; *The How of Happiness*; *The Art of Choosing*; *The Wisest One in the Room*; *Learned Optimism*; *Authentic Happiness*; *Snoop*; *Mindfulness*

Of the books on this list, *The Power of Habit* by Charles Duhigg is noteworthy in that it articulates exactly how a line of research is relevant and can be applied to actual problems, mainly in the business world. The author thoroughly explains the science in his own way and makes it perfectly clear to any nonscientist reader why it could be valuable in their work. We also recommend *The Best Place to Work* by Ron Friedman as a good example of explaining many findings in several research areas. This book is essentially a survey of social psychology and decision-making research aimed at people in business, including guidance for how this research can be applied to the workplace.

These books are good examples of "translating" findings from our science into nonscientific language. They are generally concise, and when they are not, they tell narrative stories. Crafting a description of research as a mystery or a quest makes it compelling. There is no need to oversell—our science uncovers truths about human nature that are powerful and interesting enough without being embellished. Most people have an inherent interest in hearing about basic human nature, and that alone can draw someone into conversation or make them enjoy hearing your messages. You will probably find that you prefer certain authors' styles to others. Read many, think about why your favorites are good, and use those principles in your own communications.

Know Your Audience

One of the keys to broadcasting your science is a principle that applies to any communication: Know your audience. We would complicate that in our context, however, by adding that what you really need to know is your audience's premises and how they are different than yours. We provide extensive guidance for doing this in your particular job search in Part IV, but here we give advice that can apply generally. One way to uncover mismatches is to ask your audience questions and then actively listen to the answers. Listen for what is important to them, what problems they need to solve, and their interests. Use the information you find to frame your thoughts and ideas. For example, if you talk with someone in the financial services industry, it's likely that the subject of risk management will come up. This could be in the context of technology, regulatory compliance, corporate culture (i.e., the attitudes and behaviors that are most rewarded in the company), or some other aspect of risk. If the person asks you how your science could benefit their work, you could probably strike a chord with them by explaining some ways you could reduce risk—perhaps wondering aloud how the company deals with employee development. For example, you might ask, Does the company encourage skill building alongside firm loyalty, such that employees are more motivated to protect the firm's brand rather than taking their skills and insider knowledge elsewhere?

BUILDING PROFESSIONAL PROPOSALS

This section presents a topic that might seem very specific: professional proposals. What we mean by *professional proposals*, however, is actually broad; we refer to any situation in which you will need to convince someone to support your idea or project. In many lines of work, you will present formal proposals quite often. In some of those careers, there will be lengthy forms to fill out and set formats for building proposals. In other careers, however, you might not present formal proposals very often but you will likely find yourself needing to convince others of your ideas' value or to join or support you. The principles in this section are designed to help in these more common, less formatted, but still very important situations.

"But wait," you might be wondering, "why is this topic being presented as though it's something new? I have proposed my master's and dissertation projects and have worked on a grant proposal. That qualifies as training in proposal writing!" It does, and graduate students do gain valuable experience with proposals; professional proposals, however, are often very different from academic ones.

First and foremost, most professional proposals are short. In many cases when presenting to an executive, or another decision-maker—even to your own boss—you might be given 30 minutes to present, and sometimes less. If you are scheduled for 30 minutes, you should be prepared to present your proposal in 10, because other meeting topics reliably run long and your time slot might get squeezed. In general, it's a good idea to prepare a scaled-back version of the full proposal, and even an extra-scaled-back version. You don't necessarily have to write out all the versions, but at least have an idea of what you'll do if your allotted time changes.

Of course, proposal and more general presentation formats will differ from place to place. Some jobs include long detailed proposals, much like research grant proposals. Government contract work is one example, and any field that includes bidding for big jobs against competitors is another. You might have quite extensive, and valuable, experience in building this kind of proposal! The proposals we discuss in this section are mostly relevant to business settings. In any setting, however, the ability to focus in on the most crucial information in your proposal, and the ability to communicate that information concisely, will be helpful.

When Might You Need to Present a Proposal?

What are situations in which you might need to present a proposal? Here are a few examples:

- Your boss has been asked to set up a system for gathering employee feedback on a new program that is being launched. Your boss asks you to deliver a two-slide proposal that he can include in his next presentation to executives.

- You find yourself and your team swamped with too many requests for work and are delivering results late or unreliably as a result. You have an idea for how to clean up the request and scheduling process and need to propose it to your team's leader.

- You want to partner with a local university to build an internship program, and you need to bring your HR department on board as a supporter and explain what their role would be.

- You have several ideas about how an ongoing project for which you are responsible can be better. It has been run this way a long time, since before you were hired. You are confident that certain things need to improve, but not everyone agrees. You need to marshal support for making the changes.

Key Components of a Proposal

In our experience, a few components are essential to any proposal. Clearly presenting this information has generally been successful when we need to make proposals.

- Rationale: What is the problem at hand? Why should anyone be concerned, or why does something need to be done? What might happen if nothing is done?

- Solution: What is it you are proposing to do or change?

- Risks: What might go wrong? What is typically the most worrisome aspect of similar projects, and how do you plan to mitigate them?

- Cost and schedule: What are the resources needed—funds, time, new hires, materials? What is the total cost? How long will it take?

Before you present this very brief type of proposal, you will have to work out every detail you can, of course, and probably make your case to someone who will take it up the management chain (your boss, a contact person at a client company, or a collaborator). That is when you vet every detail, project possible outcomes, shore up all supporting information, and boil down the most compelling messages. Essentially, you will do (nearly) all the work of a grant or research proposal and then present only key details in compelling ways.

One established format for proposals is SWOT, which stands for strengths, weaknesses, opportunities, and threats. Many executives are familiar with this format, and familiarizing yourself with it could be helpful (a quick Internet search will yield many resources).

TEAMWORK

Teamwork, like proposal skills, is another area in which graduate students sometimes have direct experience but often do not receive training or direct guidance. The key here, we believe, is the degree to which your outcomes depend on working with others. Psychological scientists in the academic environment are generally quite independent. As one of our PhD friends in business put it,

> There are clearly many talented social scientists who conduct valuable research and contribute to what we know about how people think, feel, and behave. The difference, however, is that social scientists are typically under no obligation to work well with others to create value in the world.

Your graduate school experience might be similar to ours in that, in your lab, you are very independent. Your success depends on your work and is rarely affected by how well you get along with, or the productivity level of, your peers. Similarly, if you have a big win or a big setback, it does not affect the careers of your labmates. This setting can work against building teamwork skills or can at least limit the opportunities to learn about working on long-term group projects with shared consequences.

Another factor working against teamwork skill building is the premise that finding weaknesses in others' ideas or work is a valuable way to make progress (mentioned in Chapter 1). It is indeed a valuable way to make progress in science, and challenges to others' conclusions in conversations and in the pages of journals can result in breakthroughs in theory. That open challenging style, however, can damage teammate relationships when it is not the norm, especially when several ideas can adequately get a job done. Arguing for a different way in these situations can cause bad feelings and can give others the impression that you lack intellectual humility (a hallmark of a good scientist; Leary et al., 2017). Of course, if you have a new idea that can improve something, you should develop it and propose it according to the norms of that workplace. But in most cases you will be entering an environment with others who have been there longer, who have specific job and/or industry expertise, and whose perspectives are as valid as yours, even if they are not based in a research literature.

Likely Teamwork Situations

There are several situations in which you might have experience working in teams. These are great experiences to talk about or list on a résumé. Here are a few possibilities:

- You might work in a lab where projects involve several graduate students; perhaps your studies take a long time and involve a lot of recruiting, and several students work on the project and then work with the data set either separately or as a team.

- You might work with several other graduate students on a project such as hosting an event or organizing a series or program.

- You might collaborate with other graduate students on a poster presentation, or even a chapter or research report.

All of these experiences will supply you with good material to discuss with interviewers when the subject of teamwork comes up.

In addition to these situations, you likely will collaborate with others on some different projects during your time at graduate school. Most of the projects will involve hierarchy, which changes the situation considerably. Normally your advisor or another faculty member or postdoc is leading, or at least participating, in the project. In this situation, there is a clear chain of command and understanding of who is making decisions and allocating tasks (or at least refereeing those decisions). The hierarchy removes most of the need to navigate relationships with peers that can sometimes be tricky and to assert yourself as or defer to a leader.

In the professional world, you might often find yourself on a team with factions who disagree on how something should be done. One faction gets their way, and the others have to yield their position. A good teammate knows when to back off their position and fall in as a follower and when it is appropriate to fight for your position—how to persuade others while still building strong relationships. This can be especially difficult if you find yourself assigned to do something with people you do not particularly like. It takes skill and experience to navigate these situations and arrive at positive outcomes as often as possible.

One of my (Patrick) most formative moments in my professional life was when my supervisor had a talk with me after a particularly contentious team discussion on how to carry out a project. She let me know that although my position might have been the best, in my attempt to prove that point, I might have come off as stubborn and too independent. I had a good record of being a role-player when I was not in the lead, but I had not figured out how to effectively take the lead when I should. Of course, it was hard to hear the constructive criticism, but I followed her guidance anyway at the next team discussion. The literature was on my side, and I was sure I had the best position. I was in fact alone in that position, but over about an hour, one by one my teammates each came to agree that my position was the best. That I "won" this debate is not what I am proud of; rather, it is that I maintained strong relationships and team cohesion with my teammates while I persuaded others of the merits of my position. That is not a skill I learned in graduate school.

Hiring managers are often keenly aware of the need for teamwork skills. They might even be aware of the stereotype that PhDs are not good at it. They might be looking for these skills particularly in your screening and interviewing process. The better case you can make for your teamwork skills, the better prepared you will be.

How to Develop Your Teamwork Skills, Starting Now

- If you are not already actively collaborating with a team, find one or make one for yourself! Volunteer for a student-led project such as a colloquium or conference organizing committee. Most departments have graduate student committees or associations, and you should actively involve yourself. You could also volunteer for local community projects or philanthropic organizations.

- Once you are on the team, actively seek out team projects that require collaboration. During these or any team projects, you will have experiences that interviewers find informative. Be conscious of the choices you make and the strategies you employ to navigate team situations, because when you are up for a new job, you will probably be asked a series of behavioral interview questions. These require you to reference your actual experiences and provide evidence. To prepare for this, you might find it useful to keep a journal of your team projects that you can go back to when crafting responses to potential behavioral interview questions. You will be amazed at the wealth of detail and the rich examples that you can draw upon to describe, for example, a time that you found yourself working with people with whom you did not agree. This is a common behavioral interviewing topic.

- Learn something from the team experience. One way to do that is to follow others, even when you do not think their way is right. Then give them the benefit of the doubt—assume they had some knowledge you did not have and try to learn why they made their decision. Objectively weigh the pros and cons of the course of action. This can help you see others' perspectives and could even help build your intellectual humility, which can be very helpful in acclimating to a new work culture. You might already have teamwork experience, but you can always try to critically evaluate your skills. How did you succeed? What challenged you and perhaps needs more work? Be open to change and honest self-evaluation.

WRAP-UP

We think communication is key to bridging premise mismatches. In fact, a major way that premises become barriers is by hampering communication. Working on the skills described in this chapter is one piece of the puzzle to working through those barriers. These skills are also great tools to use in navigating team situations. The ability to make your case concisely to teammates will be a great help in smoothing relationships and effecting persuasion.

In some cases, you might be hired into a role that obviously requires a research psychologist. In such jobs, you will not need to explain the value you bring. In other job contexts, it will benefit you to be able to make the case for your value. In either type of role, you will likely meet people for whom or find yourself in situations where you will have to quickly summarize your science or a study, and the skills in this chapter can help immensely.

TAKEAWAYS

- Several skills that graduate school normally does not teach are highly valued in many workplaces.

- Many of these skills involve communication: simplicity and brevity, broadcasting your science, preparing proposals, and teamwork.

- Resources are available for you to improve these skills during and after your graduate school training.

WHAT TO DO NOW

1. Take a journalism writing class. Two main goals here are to learn brevity and impact in writing. We believe that the main value, however, might be in learning how to zero in on the one core idea, feature that, and let go of the other details. In journalism the lesser details go toward the end of the piece. This is known as the classic inverted pyramid structure, and it's distinct from the Intro—Method—Results—Discussion format. In nonscientific communications, it can be very effective to prioritize the information this way. You can present the other detail in appendices or keep them in reserve to handle verbally.

2. Think about your favorite finding in your science—either something of your own that you are most proud of or a favorite famous finding. Describe it now in plain language. Do not describe what the researcher did at first; start by describing what it says about human behavior. Take all the time or space you need, but keep the narrative compelling. The goal here is to unspool a story, not necessarily to concisely explain a scientific contribution. Many authors in both scientific and nonscientific writing ask the reader to imagine themselves in a certain situation and think about what they would do, only to reveal what researchers have found, which is different. Try your own devices until you find ways to accurately, but compellingly, tell stories about psychology findings.

3. Take a grant proposal you or someone else wrote and translate it into a four-slide PowerPoint presentation you can give in 10 minutes. Imagine you are proposing the same project, with the same budget, to a potential funder (whether for the actual funder that was originally intended or for some imaginary philanthropic individual or organization). Capture all the impact, and cut out everything else. Get to the ask quickly. This will require that you carefully prioritize all the information. This might already be done well in the proposal—often the justification for why the proposed research is necessary appears in the first paragraph. That, however, might not be the most important information to present in your proposal. Think about why your audience will care about what you are presenting and what would most compel them to think that spending the requested money would be a good investment. (This might require that you fill in some backstory for your funders—perhaps you can imagine yourself on a reality show where you pitch business ideas.)

    Now cut it down to two slides and 5 minutes. Cut even more. It might have been excruciating to cut it down to four slides, and now you have to let go of some more information. Try letting it go, and then imagine making the presentation. Did you or the audience miss that information? What was the impact of the audience not having it?

4. Find a long-form popular science description of a line of research you like—for example, the description of habits in *The Power of Habit* by Charles Duhigg (2012). Try not to read a description that is too close to how the research would be described in a peer-reviewed journal article. Rather, find one that might strike you at first as *too* simplified.

   If you cannot find a description of research you already know, simply find one that cites the research upon which it is based, pull some of the primary research articles or meta-analyses or review articles, and acquaint yourself with the research (this might mean reading one or two review articles and some research reports). Notice these things:

   • Which of the details in the literature are important to you?

   • Which details did the popular press author retain?

   • How did the author present those details?

   • Who is the intended audience of the popular press piece?

   • Did the author successfully describe the power and/or value of the research and its real-world implications?

   • Did the author also convey any boundary conditions or important moderators?

   Now practice describing the research your own way. What would you do differently? Write out your own descriptions, and compose how you would convey them verbally. Consider the audience you are targeting, and be sure to describe the research in a way that makes it obvious to the listener or reader the value it could possibly bring to their work or life.

5. Find a listing of popular behavioral interviewing questions and study them. (We provide a starter list of resources in the Career Development Time Line.) What information do they typically aim to uncover? How might the interviewer's perspective guide how they interpret answers?

   For each question, think about how your experiences might provide materials for your answers to these questions. What experiences do you have to draw from that might be helpful? How might you reassess some of your graduate school experiences to find answers? Do you have any records to reference, such as journals or year-end or semester-end reports of your activities? Do you need to start keeping more detailed records or journals for future reference? (As already mentioned, we recommend it.) Which of the behavioral interviewing areas are most lacking for you?

Finding strong material for these topics might not be a straightforward task. At first, your experiences might not seem to include great examples of you enacting the competencies and skills called for. You might need to do some more digging and reappraising to find examples, partly because at the time, you might not have recognized the importance of certain skills outside academia, and therefore you might not have encoded them to memory. This activity should bring the importance of these skills to the forefront of your mind so that you can better document and remember relevant experiences.

PART III

ORIENTING YOURSELF TO A NEW CULTURE

Up to this point, we have considered cultural differences in the premises of academic and nonacademic contexts, and we have discussed how to examine, feature, and adapt your skills to your new workplace culture. In the next section of the book, we set about developing the materials with which you can pursue new career opportunities. Preparing and adapting these materials with your new workplace culture in mind will help you connect with people in the career paths you want to pursue.

In the next three chapters, we discuss how to effectively communicate the most relevant and powerful information about yourself and when it is crucial to do so. We take the skills you have examined and articulated and discuss how to craft them into messages that convey what you have to offer to potential hirers outside academia.

6
NEW CULTURE, NEW IDENTITY

Developing Your Professional Self

In this chapter, you begin to chart your course and collect the provisions you need for your career search. The exercises we outline here and in the rest of this book can be repeated until you land the job you want, and perhaps even after you are there. To maximize the value of this book—and really, to accomplish the goal of finding great career opportunities—you should prepare to work on the lessons we present in Chapters 6 to 11 of this volume, thoughtfully and deliberately integrating them, for as long as it takes to meet your goals.

You can expect your career search to be an iterative process. Much of what you learn will come from trial and error. You might fall flat while talking about your skills at a job fair, for example, or in an informal conversation at a networking event, but the only way to learn about how professionals in a certain field respond to your language is to use it with them and find out. Then, come back to the materials you've developed while reading this book and reword them, revise them, and reexamine any problematic premises to make them better for next time. So, go ahead and get comfortable with imperfection and tinkering. What you build as you work through the rest of this book and the job search process itself will involve many iterations.

http://dx.doi.org/10.1037/0000170-008
The Portable PhD: Taking Your Psychology Career Beyond Academia, by P. Gallagher and A. Gallagher

Iteration. Iteration is a popular concept in many professional fields. The definition is not different from what you already know (e.g., you might have done iterative model fitting), it is just used in different contexts. Whenever a team or company builds something new, they should expect to have several versions, with the first few having flaws that need to be exposed and revised. This is why there is a "version x.x.x" designation on many software products. Thus, "versioning" or "iterating" is a strategy for perfecting a product or process and improving it over time. Some people, however, might not appreciate the value of iteration and might believe it is necessary and possible to deliver something exactly right the first time. Consequently, if you can ask questions about or describe the value of iteration, perhaps as a risk-reduction strategy, that in itself can add value to your other offerings.

HOW MARKETING YOURSELF IS SIMILAR TO PRODUCT DEVELOPMENT

If you look up *product development*, you will likely find a lot of material from the consumer packaged goods industry or from other industries that build tangible objects to sell. The same principles of product development apply to any industry that aims to profitably sell things, even nontangible objects such as software or experiences. Product development is essentially designing and building something that consumers will buy.

In the context of this book, we use the term to refer to the process of defining what you have to offer and matching it to what the job market (and specifically the field where you want to work) wants. The processes of product development and marketing often overlap, and they do in our approach as well. We use the term *product development* instead of *marketing* deliberately for two reasons: first, because it can be applied to oneself as well as to building an actual new product or service (which might be a career path you pursue), and second, because we think it better captures what behavioral scientists need to do to appeal to nonacademic job markets. To elaborate, marketing often focuses on matching a finished product to consumers who would buy it; we think it will be useful for many psychologists to also focus on developing the product itself.

To illustrate how the boundaries between product development and marketing can be blurry, we want you to imagine that a car company conducts market research to learn about what consumers want and need. If they feel their product line does not match those needs, they may decide to develop a new car and engage the engineering or development department to start the design process. The company will want information about consumers' needs to guide what they build. They will get this information from the marketing team. As the new car is designed and built, the marketing team will think about how to describe its features to appeal to consumers' needs. So, the process works in two directions. In like manner, part of the process of developing yourself or your products for the market is learning what hirers or consumers want, and part is putting together your skills and abilities to build something to offer them.

The term *marketing* can sometimes have a negative connotation, especially among scientists. Sometimes it is seen as simply "selling"—persuading or, worse, coercing people into buying something they might not even want or need. There are more charitable ways to think about marketing, however, and we offer them for your consideration. Marketing can be seen as bringing to people a product or service that can improve their life in some way. Consumers are often happy to spend money on things they see as quality products or experiences that bring them fun, convenience, or solutions to a problem. Marketing professionals can work to match such consumers with products and services in a completely aboveboard and noncoercive way.

WHERE, WHEN, AND HOW WOULD PSYCHOLOGISTS USE PRODUCT DEVELOPMENT?

Psychologists who are looking to expand their career options can apply the principles and processes of product development in many ways. It might be helpful to think of three general categories of potential products to develop: yourself, your consulting offerings, and actual products for an employer.

> **Offering.** *Offering* can essentially be used interchangeably with *product*. In many cases the term *product* is not an exact fit, so *offering* is used as a more general way to refer to the things that are actually being sold. For example, a consulting firm that "sells" training programs that customers attend might refer to those programs as offerings instead of products.

Product Developing Yourself

If *product development* is designing and building a product that consumers want to buy, then by "product developing yourself" we mean finding the skills you have, building the ones you lack, and describing them in a way that matches what a hirer is looking for. One of the most basic ways to use product development is for this purpose—to position yourself competitively on the job market. Of course, the term *product development* is not typically applied to people, but we think that using its principles to apply to your professional development is very useful.

And so, in this context, the "product" is you and the "consumer" is potential hirers. There are some hirers who will understand you, the product, just by looking at your CV. These are hirers who set out to hire a behavioral scientist to conduct research and who may also have a doctoral degree. An example of this situation might be a contract research organization (CRO). If you apply for a position at a CRO, you will probably not need to do much product development on yourself. You might need to highlight some of your own research that matches the needs of the position, but there is no need to explain what value you can add as a psychologist or explain what behavioral scientists do in their training. In other positions where it is not already understood why a psychologist would be valuable (e.g., a project management position), you will need more product development.

Product Developing for Consulting

Another area in which you can employ product development is a consulting position or practice. You might want to apply for a position at a consulting firm or start your own practice as an independent consultant. In either case, you will need to identify the skills and abilities you have that hirers or clients will pay for, practice describing them in compelling ways, and be able to explain the value they can bring to many contexts.

What is consulting? Our favorite way of thinking about it is simply providing expertise or services to a client who needs, but does not have, that expertise in their company already. Perhaps a small company needs to fill a very important executive position, like chief financial officer. A small company might not have an HR professional in-house who can define the requirements of the job, perform a search for good candidates, expertly choose the best candidates, and then perform assessments and interviews to find the best candidate. That company could hire a consulting firm to do all that work for them. That would probably make more sense than hiring an HR professional permanently when there is no need—instead, hiring a consultant, even for $50,000 or more, could be an economically sound strategy. As another example, a company might have an important management team, but they are not producing or working well together. They might need an outside facilitator to come in for a few days, meet with the team, uncover problems, and train team members how better to work together. If that company does not have a team in-house who can do this work, the small expense (which could be in the neighborhood of $10,000–$50,000) of an outside consultant can be a wise investment.

Normally it takes a long time to build a practice from scratch. If consulting is a career path that interests you, you could have a considerable head start by beginning as early as possible in graduate school. Even if you are interested in consulting for a firm, any experience you can gain while in graduate school will still be valuable in your job search. In the following chapters we provide more direct information about how to use a product development type approach to build a consulting practice.

Product Development as a Job

The third general category in which product development principles are important is the traditional area of product development itself. In this scenario, you might be hired to join a company's product development team. You might also do product development work as part of a research and development department. In this position, you might focus on any or all of the components of the product development process. We list those components in Chapter 7.

A behavioral scientist could contribute to product development by conducting original research among consumers to discover their needs or desires from certain products. This could take the form of very traditional psychology research, where there is a lab and other psychologists with backgrounds similar to yours. More likely, you will find yourself working with, or on, a market research team, which conducts studies around such topics as consumers' impressions of current brands, their affective responses to new promotional materials or messages, or their likelihood to buy in different contexts.

Another role a psychologist could play in product development is to advise a product team about how to configure product features based on how people think, feel, and behave. For example, a company might be developing software products to help children learn basic math, and you could be hired as a subject matter expert on childhood development to advise the team on how to configure game rewards, how to present problems, or when to present more or less difficult problems to users.

A third role a psychologist might fill in product design is in creating products based directly in psychology. Childhood reading or math apps are good examples of this type of product. Other examples include positive psychology and meditation apps and websites that help consumers build healthful habits. You could be hired as part of a team that develops products like these, or you could come up with your own idea and build a startup around it. The latter path is much more complicated, but if entrepreneurship is exciting to you, it might be a great career option. In this area, just like building a consulting practice, an early start can help you get up and running faster after graduation.

WRAP-UP

We believe that one of the primary reasons psychology PhDs struggle to find fulfilling careers outside of academia is that they might not be able to identify, describe, and present the value they offer to potential hirers. The premises of academia mismatching the premises of other fields is the major barrier that causes this disconnect. The principles and practices of product development compose the framework we propose for psychologists to overcome that barrier.

Product development, in the sense that we use the term, is identifying what you have to offer and packaging and presenting it in ways that attract potential hirers or clients. Applying it to your preparation for the job market, to your actual career search, and even to your work once you do land a job can be the key to success outside academia.

Whether the product is you, your consulting offerings, or an actual product, prepare to loop back to the beginning more than once. Often, the place where you start your second or subsequent iteration of development won't be the same place you started the last time—because you are constantly learning from experience (and mistakes).

TAKEAWAYS

- From here on out, your career search will be an iterative process of product development and exploring the job market.

- Product development is the process of building offerings that hirers or consumers will want (to hire or buy).

- You can take several routes with product development, but perhaps the most fundamental is developing how to articulate the value you can bring to any professional context.

WHAT TO DO NOW

1. Read some Implications sections of research articles, and look for ways that authors suggest their findings might be used or applied. Many articles suggest that their findings could be used by therapists in treatment. Others suggest ways that their findings can be used in education or in policy. Find some of these ideas and actually think through how they could be made real. Could there be a business opportunity there? Can you see how you would instruct people or build a guide to apply any findings in an applied scenario?

   This might be really hard—you may have no idea how a given industry works—but explore that industry and try to find out. Explore the marketplace that might include related products or services. Take note of any ideas you might have, regardless of their sophistication level and regardless of how grandiose they might be. Often a big idea can be broken down into smaller parts, and just one of those smaller parts can be an entire business.

   The idea here is not to come up with a finished business plan. Instead, it is to help you start thinking and generating ideas. Let your mind speculate and imagine. Later, after reading and practicing the activities in the rest of this book, you can come back to some of these ideas and be more specific about actually proposing them, or at least discussing them in an interview or informal conversations with people in your network. For now, simply apply your creativity to thinking up ideas that are not theories of human behavior or hypothesis tests, but instead things or services people might want to buy.

2. Think of a product or a marketing message that made you think, "They have this all wrong. Research clearly shows that if they had done x, it would be much better." It might be an app that has a frustrating design detail, a feature of an appliance that misses an opportunity to capitalize on a common habit or basic cognitive process, or a 15-second video ad that could have appealed to viewers in a different way. What would you tell the designers? What should have been different, and on what research is your idea based?

   The purpose of this exercise is to help you consider the wide range of possibilities for applying psychology to the world. Looking increasingly for these instances can help you to think about new and diverse ways that the subject in which you are an expert—behavioral science

literature and practice—can be applied to things that people make and
consume.

3. Check out Happify.com, Limeade.com, beworks.com, or zenzi.com. Read
   through the pages, learn about what they offer, and find the prices of the
   products they offer. What did they do to build this business? How did
   they translate psychological science into a sellable service? What insights
   can you extract from that—that is, can you take anything they did, define
   some general guidelines or rules, and then apply those rules or guidelines to another area of psychology? Who would buy it? How would you
   frame its value—what would consumers be receiving for their money?
   Why would it be worth their money?

7
COMMUNICATING YOUR STORY

The Building Blocks

For a behavioral scientist to be viable on the general job market, potential hirers need to understand why they might want to have one around. It is up to you to provide that explanation. You have to convince yourself first and then figure out how to speak about it so anyone can understand. If you do a good-enough job, not only will those around you understand what you can do but potential employers will feel like they need to hire you. This chapter presents a method for doing that.

If you have not been in a nonacademic job interview or other situation where you needed to explain the value you add (or could add), it might not be clear to you why all this preparatory work is necessary. When you find yourself struggling to communicate that you really can contribute something valuable to a project, or when you think you explained it well in an interview but do not receive a call back, the value of this preparation work might become obvious. Smart, accomplished, benevolent people can be completely mystified about what a behavioral scientist can do if there is a premises mismatch.

Because it is vitally important that hirers understand why they need you, we recommend spending plenty of time on the steps in this chapter. We state

http://dx.doi.org/10.1037/0000170-009
The Portable PhD: Taking Your Psychology Career Beyond Academia, by P. Gallagher and A. Gallagher

again here that this should be done iteratively, or in cycles. You can "test out" the material you develop as you prepare for your job search, then return to the steps in this chapter to revise and improve your materials based on the results. We truly believe that psychological researchers' chances of success in the general job market (especially in competing for the *best* positions) can suffer without this kind of preparation. Therefore, time spent developing these aspects of your professional identity is a wise investment.

ARTICULATING WHAT YOU BRING TO AN EMPLOYER

The following list presents the concepts that are the building blocks of your story, or at least the professional story that you present to prospective employers. We describe and discuss each concept in the following pages. You can consider each one a step to complete, but you do not have to do them in any particular order. You might even find that some lend themselves to being completed simultaneously.

We certainly have not set out to craft new or authoritative definitions of the terms presented in this chapter. We recommend that you delve into other sources for additional perspectives on any of these terms that particularly interest you. Our goal is to discuss the following concepts as important components in preparing you for a nonacademic job.

- Vision
- Mission
- Market need and positioning
- Customers and segments
- Value propositions (or "value props")
- Differentiators

In addition to these six, there are other components that go to a finer level of detail—for example, *messaging* or crafting elevator pitches. They do not appear in this chapter's list because we are mainly concerned here with the rough translation of your story. We devote Chapter 8 to the elements that provide finesse.

Vision Statement

What changes do you want to effect in the world through your work? What is the bigger purpose you want to pursue in your professional life? What improvement, solution, or change do you want to make in the world? These are some of the questions that can help you design a vision statement. A *vision statement* is a postcard from your end state—what the world will look like if you accomplish what you want to professionally.

We admit: Vision statements can sound silly. They can sound unrealistic and hokey. But a good one can be very useful. And, if it truly captures a higher calling that you are pursuing in your professional life, it can be inspirational and clarifying for you, not to mention for your potential hirers.

A good vision statement should be concise and aspirational. It should capture what you really care about and should accurately reflect the high-level outcome(s) you are pursuing in your work. We recommend looking up examples—they can help you see how you might define your vision. Some typical examples of vision statements might sound like "To build a company that improves the lives of others." "A world in which everyone is treated equally." "A life of dignity for those in poverty." These are quite general, and they can serve very well as guideposts for what you are trying to accomplish.

You can craft a vision statement for yourself, or for a company you want to build. Corporations are normally where vision statements are found—most of the examples you find will likely be company vision statements. If, in fact, you are planning to build a consulting practice or any other company, you can and should craft a vision statement for it. Even if you are simply preparing yourself for the job market, we recommend articulating one that applies to you as a professional behavioral scientist.

The most valuable purpose of a vision statement in your career search is to help guide your thinking and communicating in important situations. When you are chatting with network contacts, talking with a hirer in a job interview, or even meeting and working with people on the job, a vision statement can help you communicate with others. You may not recite your vision word for word, but you might reference it to respond to certain questions. You might find it particularly useful for "why" questions. (Why did you choose to leave academia? Why are you interested in working at our company? Why are you here at this event?) If your vision itself is a bit abstract for the question, you might at least reference it in your mind, and then answer the question based on it. For example, if your vision is "A life of dignity for those in poverty," and you are asked in an interview why you are leaving academia, you might refer to your vision and answer, "Helping those in poverty is personally important to me, and I think I can do more towards that goal in a position like this one."

An important consideration here is how concrete to be in different situations. A vision statement can be quite abstract, and some audiences, such as a job interviewer, might be looking for something concrete when they ask a question about your motivation or your goals. It might be helpful to think of your vision statement as a guidepost—not something to explicitly share but something to help guide your thinking for bigger long-term questions.

What to do to start on your vision statement? Look up some examples, become comfortable with what a vision statement is, and draft one. Start thinking about it now—once you have a draft, think it over as you continue your studies and your other preparations for your career. As you picture the person you will be in the future, and as you make decisions about which career paths you would like to pursue, think about what is most important to you. Revise your vision statement accordingly. Unless you are already crystal clear about your purpose on this earth and your career direction (a rare situation for anyone), this will likely be an ongoing process.

Some example vision statements can be found at commercial websites that provide consulting on business building; for nonprofits, you can go to the Top Nonprofits website (see Top Nonprofits, n.d.). We also found that Internet image searches yield a plethora of easy-to-access vision and mission statements.

Mission Statement

A *mission statement* typically describes what you actually want to *do* and how you do it in order to carry out your vision. It is more concrete and describes the actions you want to take or the products you want to deliver. A mission statement for a science-based employee engagement consulting firm might be "To apply behavioral science to increase employee engagement and improve clients' business outcomes." A mission statement in the health care industry might be: "To improve doctor–patient relationships, and ultimately patients' health, by applying psychological science findings to clinical interactions." These are much more specific and more precisely communicate your role to the audience (or what you would like your role to be). We recommend again that you search for more examples—they will give you a strong idea of what to aim for and what to avoid.

You might see mission statements on individuals' professional profiles on corporate websites or social media. You might also see them on generic résumés. Mission statements, or versions of them (i.e., Objective statements), can be effective ways to inform readers about what kind of professional you are, or what positions you are interested in pursuing.

A word of caution here: When searching for a job, your personal mission statement, if it is visible, should not be so specific that it would turn away recruiters or hirers. For example, if you are applying for a general HR support position, your LinkedIn profile should probably not include a mission statement that includes specific areas. If the hiring manager reads that your mission is "To apply scientific survey methodology to accurately measure employee attitudes," they might conclude that you are not a good fit for a position that involves duties other than just that role and delete your résumé. It is likely more prudent to post something broader (but still informative) on publicly visible platforms. For example, a "purpose" or "mission" on your LinkedIn profile might read, "I apply behavioral science to measure and improve business processes."

Like a vision statement, a mission statement can help you generate answers to an unexpected, surprising, or hard-to-answer question. In these situations, you can refer to your vision and/or mission statements and give an answer that would move the problem toward the end state articulated in your vision or describe how you would solve the problem in accordance with your mission. As a generic example, suppose that in an interview you were unexpectedly asked how you would approach a specific problem at a company (one you could not have learned about beforehand). Your mission statement might include your intent to apply your scientific training, and you can compose your answer based on that guidepost: How would you approach the problem as a scientist in your lab if it were a research question? Your answer might begin, "I would first want to look at the data. I would want to know variables x, y, and z. If there are no data, my next step would be to see if a research study was feasible to collect those data. . . ."

In addition to guiding your communication with potential hirers, mission and vision statements can be very helpful in guiding your own creativity or motivation. For example, if you find yourself stuck in a rut while trying to develop a product or a company, or if you are having trouble choosing between two possible career paths, you can refer to your vision and/or mission statements for guidance. "If what I truly want to do in life is _____, then what I need to do here is _____."

At some point while composing statements, many people find it hard to differentiate between vision and mission statements. When you are trying to compose them, they can often run together or start sounding similar. A shorthand way to tell them apart is this: A *vision statement* is the state of things at the end of what you want to do (the "postcard from the end state"). It is your end goal for what the world should look like. A *mission statement* is the actions you are here to do, what you do day to day, or the tangible product you make to achieve that end state.

Ultimately, precise definitions of these terms do not matter much. We think the exercise of thinking the differences through can help you compose and remember your vision and mission. The most important outcome, however, is for you to have guideposts that will be useful for you in any situation. You can share your personal vision statement with a potential hirer, you can refer to your mission statement to focus your tasks, you can use both to answer tough interview questions—as long as you have them to draw upon, they will be serving their purpose in your career search.

A final note on your mission and vision statements: As important as it is to make them concise and accurate, do not be afraid to revise them or to throw them out entirely and start over when needed. You will probably need several versions as you go through your career search and even after you have started your career.

What to do to write your mission statement? Simply this: Write a draft, and plan to revise over the coming months and years. Your mission statement will include more concrete actions and objectives, so it might be helpful to work on your mission and vision statements in parallel and to work out the different purposes and uses of the two statements.

Example mission statements can be found in many of the same resources as vision statements. Two articles that provide examples are authored by Lindsay Kolowich (2019) and Susan Ward (2018).

Market Need and Positioning

Market need refers to something that potential customers out there in the world are seeking. It is a deficit that you can help fill. If you are a developmental psychologist with program evaluation skills and the product you are developing is program evaluation consulting services, the market need would be companies that are implementing programs or projects and must track and measure them but have no in-house experts to do so. This information goes hand in hand with describing your product and how your product will meet the need.

Potential investors or sponsors in a new product or venture typically want to know the market need for new products. This could be a pitfall for unprepared entrepreneurs: If you cannot make the case that a need exists or can be created, even a brilliant product could fail to launch. Consumers may not be aware of the need; you could provide products or services to solve a problem that consumers do not realize they have. For example, perhaps after learning how marketing firms typically handle a certain type of market research, you identify a way to get more insight from their data. Your product could be an application that processes and analyzes those data to deliver that insight. Marketing firms could be completely unaware of this "need," but if you build a convincing case around it, many could be willing to pay for your product.

You may not have to identify a need that no one else is filling. It could be a need for which many companies offer products but there is still such strong demand that your product or service could be viable.

If you are the product and you are looking for a position at an established company, the market need would be the skills or perspective you can bring that they do not currently have. If you can provide employee surveys, for example, you might need to make the case for why a client would need your survey services specifically, when they can get employee surveys from 100 other companies. Thinking in terms of their need—what they lack that you can provide—can help you articulate your value in terms they will appreciate. To do so, you will need to understand the current state of things at a potential client company (as best you can). In other words, thinking in terms of market need can help you bridge a premises gap.

How will you present your product to potential customers in relation to others who offer similar products or services? Will you offer a lower price than the market giant? Will you specialize in only one type of company as customers? Will you be the most scientific of the field of competitors? These questions can help you determine your positioning. *Positioning* refers to where your product stands when potential customers are surveying the marketplace. Knowing your positioning will help you focus your efforts on developing the best possible product for the right customers and the most appropriate and effective promotional strategy. For example, if your position is as the best low-priced scientific consultant, you should probably not spend too much time developing marketing materials for large corporations—your target market is most likely smaller companies with lower budgets. Determining your positioning can help you clarify what offerings you develop, your pricing, who your customers will be, and other important concepts.

How does positioning apply to you if you are seeking employment at an established firm? Consider how you compare to other types of people whom the firm might consider for the job. Perhaps you are the most rigorously scientific, or the one who brings the most relevant experience on top of the PhD. There could be no way to anticipate what the competition looks like; however, you might learn about them in an interview, and thinking through your positioning beforehand can help you have a comment at the ready to pique a hirer's interest. For example, imagine that a developmental psychologist applies for a position at an educational program evaluation agency. She learns about the agency's strengths and weaknesses by asking about them during the interview. She might position herself to address one of the weaknesses by highlighting that she has more expertise about differences in how children learn at each age, which could inform new ways of conducting evaluations.

Positioning is another area in which we encourage you to expect change. You might set out into the marketplace with one idea of your positioning and find after some time that a different position might work better for you. The more you think about it, the more flexible you can be.

What to do now to define the market need you aim to fill and articulate your positioning? For now, just start generating ideas—with the expectation, of course, that you will revise those ideas with increased exposure to the market. You might learn, for example, after aiming for a job in the sports and fitness industry, that most of the people who perform the job functions you want to do have PhDs in sports psychology. You might be a social psychologist who specializes in group dynamics. Through interviewing and meeting people in the industry, you might find that social psychological theories of motivation are very interesting to people in the industry. You might then brush up on that literature and position yourself as someone who can bring a unique angle to this area.

Customers and Segments

Doubtless you will find that as you are working through your market needs and positioning, your mind wanders to the people who will have the need, or who will be your customers. This endeavor includes not only identifying who will pay for your product (or pay you a salary) but also understanding who they are, what they care about, and of course what they need. In other words, understanding who your customers are can help you understand their premises.

Prospective information about potential future customers—that is, defining who will buy your product—is mainly relevant to new product or business development, but it can also help psychological scientists prepare for the job market. In the context of a new business or product, identifying who your customers will be is a central feature of a product or business proposal. Essentially, there must be some convincing evidence that people out there will spend their money on what you are developing. In the context of a job search, you will need to identify the types of companies, departments, or individuals who will or should be interested in hiring you.

The other main area of customer analysis—studying current customers—is often done for products already on the market. The goal here is to understand the concerns, interests, and opinions of the people who already are spending money on your product or on similar products so that product features and/or persuasive communications can be designed to appeal to them. In Chapters 9 and 10, we discuss strategies for exploring potential career paths and understanding the people you will deal with on each journey.

Segments are subgroupings of your customers. Companies offering products that appeal to wide varieties of people often want to produce different product features or advertising to appeal more powerfully to their customers. For example, nearly every U.S. adult uses a cell phone. Phone manufacturers and service providers likely have broken up that massive customer base into useful segments, such as college students, low-income families, and older couples with adult children, based on their budgets, usage habits, or other factors. Companies probably have slightly different strategies for advertising to these groups, and those differences are designed to make the advertising more appealing and persuasive to all customers.

Segments can be defined by anything that meaningfully differentiates groups of people in terms of their behaviors—often their buying behaviors, but also sometimes other variables such as leisure-time activities, hobbies, or interests. As applied to developing a career, segmenting can take the form of identifying three or four industries or job types that interest you and preparing résumés and other materials to fit each one. If you go into market research, you will likely find that this application of segmenting is a bit loose, but we think that applying the concept in this way might be quite useful for your purposes now.

Here again, you might find it difficult to separate thinking about who your customers are from thinking about your market needs and positioning. For the most part, that is just fine—you will need to think about both, and they are naturally intertwined. However, we encourage you to take the time to understand the differences between the approaches. More clarity in each area can only help you communicate your value.

What to do now to start defining your customers and segments? No surprise here: Get to know the concepts, and develop some rough ideas with the expectation of revising them. One way to do this is to spend time thinking about the audiences you will try to appeal to—certain types of industries or companies, certain departments that can appear in many companies, or certain potential clients or customers. The main goal is to become more fluent thinking in those terms.

Value Propositions

A *value proposition* (or its cooler street name, value prop) is something of value that you bring to the table. For example, the main value proposition of a fast-food restaurant is predictable food served quickly and at a low price. In the context of a career search, identifying your value propositions can help guide what you feature on a résumé or in a job interview. Practicing how to communicate your value props can be very helpful when an interviewer, or even someone in an unexpected context, quizzes you about what you can offer.

The ideal value prop is something that is instantly understandable and compelling—something that causes the listener to take notice and feel as if they need what you have. You can compose some of your value props generically so that they apply in almost any context, and others will need to be tailored to a specific industry or job role. Here are several value props that just about any PhD scientist might claim, adapted slightly to match the context:

- Knowledge of 140 years of scientific research into human thoughts, emotions, and behavior (a psychologist is familiar with about 140 years of research—the field began formally in the late 1870s)

- Fluency in the scientific literature that can be brought to bear on many business problems

- Expertise in designing, executing, analyzing, and reporting research projects

- Expertise in the mechanisms of human behavior that marketing or business-trained people cannot provide

Here are several examples of how these and other more specific value props might be described on a résumé or in conversation:

- "I can provide deep insight into core drivers of people's behavior—motivation, emotion, personality, and other drivers."

- "I have innovative, sophisticated research ideas and statistical analytical skills that expand the new knowledge you can gain from your testing program."

- "My survey expertise will help tap into your employees' true attitudes and feelings and then generate concrete, actionable recommendations for what to do to improve where needed."

- "I bring deep knowledge of research into how children's brains retain information and how that process differs across the life span."

- "I have expertise in the most cutting-edge research methodologies that can push your product development past the competition."

These value props descriptions should be phrases or short sentences that anyone can understand right away. They will be even more effective if they are matched to the language of the industry you are targeting. You will probably not present them by saying, "My main value prop is that I can . . .";

it will likely be more appropriate to answer questions or bring them up in conversation in a form similar to the preceding examples. Of course, you should use whatever style is most effective in the context. You may find the idea of this type of direct self-promotion distasteful. We encourage you to realize that these statements are, in fact, true of you, and although they may sound bold in the academic context, they are normative in many contexts outside academia. Remember the goal: Hirers need to know why you add value to their organization.

The concept of value props is straightforward, but developing and articulating them well can be a long, iterative process with many fits and starts. You might think that you have crafted a killer message that would motivate any hirer to offer you employment on the spot, only to find that it falls flat when you try it. This might be, as you have probably already identified, the result of a premise mismatch that you did not anticipate. As a result, the identification of your value props and the way to communicate them will most likely be an exercise in repeated composition and revision. It is, however, perhaps the most valuable material you will have when it comes time to craft messages (covered in Chapter 8) to build a résumé, write a cover letter, or have an impromptu conversation with a professional connection.

What to do now. As for how to start articulating your value props, our advice here is a bit different from the other concepts in this chapter. You can make a lot of progress on this process right now. In fact, if you have ever drafted a résumé, you have already started this exercise by writing up your skills in terms that help readers to understand the value you offer. We will say again, however, that you should expect to revise how you phrase and describe your value props once you identify the particular premises, and the potential mismatches, in the fields in which you want to work. Even with that revision in mind, you can cover a lot of ground now by listing all the skills you have and practicing articulating them in terms of value propositions.

Differentiators

Differentiators are closely related to value props. They are aspects or features of your offering that set you apart from your competitors. A differentiator is why a customer would pick you or your product over other options on the market.

In the context of a career search, a differentiator would answer the question "Why would I hire a psychologist for this job instead of someone with business experience or training?" Similarly, once on the job, you might refer to your differentiators when someone asks, "What is a psychologist doing here?" This question will be salient on the minds of your new coworkers. Many of them will conflate your educational background with Freudian theory, assume you were trained as a psychotherapist, or half-jokingly ask if you are analyzing them right now.

For an example of how a differentiator might be used in an interview situation, we use one of the value props just described. If a psychologist is asked why she or he would be a valuable addition to a marketing team, or more directly, why she or he should be hired over a marketing professional, the answer could be, "The average marketing professional can provide really good insight into some typical drivers of purchase behaviors. A psychologist can bring deep insight into core drivers of people's behavior—motivation, emotion, personality, and social factors. Your competitors *all* have market researchers, but do they have a psychologist?" This example is admittedly heavy-handed; you would want to capture this idea in a response that feels comfortable to you. You are competing with individuals who may have a more traditional or obviously relevant career path, so you will need to make your unique value known explicitly.

A similar concept to differentiators is the unique selling proposition (or USP). The USP can be thought of as a blend of the value proposition and differentiators. The USP is the value you offer that no one else can. This concept is perhaps most relevant for developing brand-new products or services instead of developing new or better products or services that customers are already familiar with, and it might be more difficult to apply it to your career search. If you spend time developing your value propositions and differentiators and becoming comfortable speaking about them, we are confident you will be ready.

Unless you are already familiar with the other products, services, or candidates in the markets you want to work, you will probably have to rely on the work you do in Chapters 9 and 10 to define your differentiators. For now, get to know the concepts, make an early attempt at writing down your differentiators, and look forward to the learning process of revising them!

WRAP-UP

The concepts in this chapter, and the practice you put in to learn and apply them, constitute important preparatory work that you will find valuable as you transition from academia to a career outside it. This work can put you on the path to identifying and dealing with premises that might act as barriers to finding a fulfilling career.

There is another benefit to your work on these concepts. One of the biggest hesitations that potential employers might have about you is whether you can function outside of the well-defined world of academia, surrounded by people who do not have your expertise and training. If you can speak effectively about your skills and what you have to offer in a job interview, and if you are familiar with the concepts in this chapter, that will be a big help in overcoming a major barrier.

TAKEAWAYS

- Familiarizing yourself with the basic concepts of product development and marketing can be valuable in preparing for your career.

- Writing vision and mission statements can help you understand what you really want to accomplish and guide many decisions and conversations in your career search.

- Thinking critically about the needs and your positioning in the market can clarify how you present yourself and focus your materials.

- Your value propositions are core materials you can refer to for much of your career search.

WHAT TO DO NOW

1. Listen to the Ted Radio Hour segment with Sam Sternberg (see National Public Radio & TED, 2016). Listen carefully around these time points: 5:55, 8:33, 9:14, 10:28. (These are time points in the segment on the NPR show website, not Sternberg's actual TED Talk video.)

   a. Can you describe what he and his collaborators are doing with the new technology they developed? Why he is doing it? What went on in his lab during his PhD work?

   b. Can you identify his vision? Mission? Market need?

   Almost every concept in this chapter can be found in his talk and in his interview with show host Guy Raz (even if slightly different terms are used). This is a very good example of how academic research can be described in a way that is informed by product development and marketing concepts. Of course, the research Sternberg conducted could be seen as much more translatable to commercial applications, which might make it easier to do this work. We believe, however, that nearly any psychological research can add value to some aspects of life. We bet you do too. It is up to you to decide how to use your vision, goals in life, and creativity follow this path.

2. Build a website.

You can start building a website by drafting the content for just a few pages. This exercise forces you to make concrete the messages and ideas you are working on and to think about people actually seeing it. If you are thinking of starting a business or building a consulting practice, build a site for it, if only a first draft. Many DIY website builders are available for a minimal cost.

Even if you do not see the need for a website in your career aspirations, going through this exercise can still be useful, because it forces you to answer several questions about aspects such as your value propositions and differentiators. Who would come to your website? What are they looking for? What can you offer them? Why would they click on anything? What can you tell them that would drive them to click on something?

If you do want to start building a website, the DIY builders have templates and often include tips about how to create a good site. There are also many resources about the basics of web design if you need help making compelling pages. These resources can continue pushing you to answer questions about what you have to offer and who might be interested in it.

8 COMMUNICATING YOUR STORY IN A NEW CULTURE

Now that you have spent some time thinking about the key concepts of marketing and how you can use them to prepare for your career search, you are in great shape to compose content. By *content*, we mean any written or spoken material that will fill up your cover letters, résumés, websites, social media channels, job interview responses, and informal conversations in any professional venue. (Of course, you can and should use the résumé you worked on after Chapter 3 or any materials you might have already drafted for nonacademic applications.)

The need for scientists to generate communications that describe what they do in simple terms has received attention, and indeed some schools have programs that help students develop these skills. We encourage you to take advantage of any resources to which you have access to help develop how you speak and write about your skills and abilities. Our focus in this chapter is to introduce these content types from the perspective of the premises approach and to help you start composing them using the raw materials you developed in Chapter 7.

http://dx.doi.org/10.1037/0000170-010
The Portable PhD: Taking Your Psychology Career Beyond Academia, by P. Gallagher and A. Gallagher

When going from the building blocks to the particulars of your professional story, you'll want to devote your attention to the following:

- Messaging
- One-sentence statement
- Elevator pitch
- Longer descriptive passage

What is the ultimate value of developing the aforementioned types of content? It is having what you need on hand when you need it. When it's time to make that 27th version of your résumé to submit to yet another job listing, you will have an inventory of content from which you can cut and paste. When an acquaintance mentions a job opening at her company and learns you are interested, and she asks what she should tell the hirer about you, you'll have a few relevant, memorable phrases to give her. The goal is not to generate misleading or hyperbolic language but rather to accurately and compellingly describe your value propositions, differentiators, special skills, and other important information and to be able to quickly adapt it to various opportunities that arise.

MESSAGING

Messaging is a set of quick, powerful statements that clearly capture key points you want to communicate. It is a concept you might hear in the fields of marketing, public relations (PR), or communications. It is narrower than the term *content*; content can refer to anything from bullet points to proposal presentations to books. Messaging is normally used to refer to a concerted effort to boil down some ideas or concepts into prioritized, easy-to-communicate points.

The results of an exercise in messaging are often referred to as a set of talking points. Talking points might be distributed by a company's marketing department to its salespeople so that they can highlight the most important features of the company's products or use the most persuasive language. They can take the form of a few phrases or longer sentences or can be prioritized lists that highlight the messages that should be invoked for different audiences.

What might messaging for a psychologist on the job market look like? Over our careers we have developed messaging for several job roles and audiences. Here are some examples:

1. I study the factors that make people truly fulfilled and motivated at work.
2. I solve business problems by applying behavioral science.

3. We apply behavioral science to make communications clearer and more persuasive.
4. I help groups work more productively using the science of group processes.
5. Team building is the perfect place for a psychologist because of the decades of research into how groups work together and change.
6. I am drawn to this organization because I want to apply my training to work with people directly rather than in a lab.

At first, these statements may appear similar to your value propositions. Note that they differ, however, in that they are more general, used earlier in the job search process, and demonstrate your relevance in a more global way. Your messages, or talking points, should be accurate and adapted to the context. For example, the third example is quite unspecific and might be appropriate only as the most general description of someone in a wide-ranging role. The first example briefly describes what a researcher of employee engagement does, but for audience members who are familiar with the concept, it might be uninformative. The fourth example could be included in a social media profile. Your list might grow to be 10, 15, or more talking points, and if you are interested in more than one career field, you might have several partially overlapping sets of talking points.

You are probably aware that canned statements can sound insincere. When you rattle off something that is clearly memorized, especially if it does not quite fit the context, it can often work against you even if the ideas are sound. It is normal in some contexts, however, to have a rehearsed way of describing what you can do. When a potential hirer asks you to describe what you do "in a nutshell," for example, a polished response is probably expected. You should memorize your talking points but not shoehorn them into conversations where they don't belong. You should know your talking points well enough to be nimble in adapting them to the specific context and/or conversation. If your talking points genuinely capture what you believe about yourself and your goals, then they will probably not sound contrived.

The Value of Messaging

Having a good set of messages or talking points is very useful in organizing your catalogue of skills, abilities, value propositions, and all other points that would interest hirers, investors, or buyers. Once all those points, ideas, or concepts are boiled down into a manageable set of messages, you can quickly run through them in your mind, or have the best ones at the ready when put on the spot.

Talking points can also guide the thoughts and ideas that represent you in public forums such as social media. Profile information, the subject matter of your posts, and the sources you follow might all be guided by the content of your messaging. A social media presence is not strictly necessary to be a competitive job candidate, but hirers routinely look at social media to learn about candidates formally or informally. You might want to build a presence in selected venues (LinkedIn should be your first priority), and your messaging can become an excellent source of material. If you already have presences on social media that you use for other purposes, now might be the time to shift your activity to supporting your job search. The material and networks that you build on social media can contribute to an overall image of you that hirers can see.

Having a set of messages is also extremely valuable in steering conversations. Have you ever unexpectedly run into an esteemed researcher in your field, had a conversation, and then afterward thought, "Oh no! I forgot to tell him about that great result we found on that one study!" Knowing the points you need to make, and recognizing the situations in which you need to make them, helps you avoid missed opportunities. If you are in a job interview and you have not had the chance to hit some of your strongest points, you should recognize that and steer the conversation to a point that allows you to make them.

Talking points are not fully effective if they are not "premise proofed." A talking point is not just one of your value propositions, it is a value proposition stated in language that is effective for the audience. If you have not examined your points for potentially problematic academic premises, or adequately matched them to the language of your audience, they might not effectively convey. Trying out your talking points with various audiences will help you craft the best way to say or write them.

How to Generate Messaging

- First, build a document with bullet points to fill in your messages.

- Then start with the work you did in Chapter 7. Choose a value proposition that you articulated.

- Examine it for academic premises that might get in the way of its effectiveness—for example, does it imply that laboratory research is more valuable than effective application? Does it assume that the audience accepts the scientific process as a gold standard? Those or other premises might not be appropriate for your new context.

- Now try applying the shortening and simplifying skills we discussed in Chapter 5 of this volume. Reduce the value proposition down to its essential message and then use nonscientific language to describe it.

- Finally, iterate. This revision step can be done only through trial and error. Try your messages on friends and family or on other students. A great time to try them is when you meet people and they ask you what you do. Eventually, you should try them in professional contexts. You can be explicit in asking for feedback, or just try them at appropriate moments and see if they excite anyone or kill the conversation (or worse, cause eyes to glaze over). This will be an ongoing process, and you might even continue developing your messages throughout your career.

ONE-SENTENCE STATEMENT

A one-sentence statement needs to orient the audience to who you are and why you are there. If you've ever attended a workshop or seminar in which you needed to introduce yourself, you probably recognize the value of practicing your one-sentence statement. It is especially important in contexts where there are few or no other scientists working. There are many job situations in which having a concise, relevant 5-second statement about yourself can be important. You might be working at your job and run into an executive, meet someone unexpected at a job interview, or be networking at a local meeting and get briefly introduced to a well-connected person. In these situations, a 1-minute elevator pitch can be too much, but you still need to convey something compelling.

An effective one-sentence statement can be complicated by the potential communication barriers that premises can present. For an academic working or looking to work in the nonacademic world, an effective, concise one-sentence statement is not easy to accomplish. Thinking about it beforehand can really pay off.

After working on your messaging or talking points, your one-sentence statement should be quite easy to write. It is essentially one or maybe two of your messages, chosen to be most relevant to the situation. Meeting an executive probably calls for a statement that you're a behavioral scientist and what you are working on. If you can find language that strikes a chord with your audience, they might ask you more, get to know you better, and remember you. If you do not raise any interest, the opportunity could pass.

This statement should be fluid—that is, it should not be a canned sentence you repeat any time you meet someone. There could be an extra point that you include in interviews, a version that is better for casual nonprofessional contexts, and another version that is useful in networking contexts. Once you have organized your materials into messaging, it should be easier to know what points to try to cover in each situation. It will also be much easier to know what works once you start trying your statements with people and getting feedback.

Also, your one-sentence statement does not have to be exactly one sentence. It can technically be two or three sentences—the goal is that it needs to be an appropriate length to be used in a quick introduction.

ELEVATOR PITCH

An *elevator pitch* is a very short presentation of what you do, what you're offering, or what you're asking for. It is normally expected to be less than 1 minute, but it could range up to 2 minutes. The elevator pitch comes from the entrepreneurship world, and the idea is if you are building a business (or a new project in an existing company) and you find yourself in an elevator with an investor or CEO, you need to have a pitch for your project that will interest her in the 40 or 50 seconds it takes the elevator to reach her floor.

Normally, an elevator pitch includes a proposition—a proposal or an ask for investment, for example. The concept has broadened, however, to refer to any quick and compelling passage that accurately and interestingly describes a project. In these contexts, it might be called an "elevator speech" instead of a pitch. Many job seekers are advised to have an elevator speech ready that describes who they are and the job they are seeking.

If your desired career is in entrepreneurship (building businesses), you should absolutely have an elevator pitch ready. You will likely find yourself in many situations where there is a potential investor or champion who could help you. Many other careers involve proposing new products or projects internally in a company, and an elevator pitch will be very valuable in those contexts as well.

An effective elevator pitch should paint a picture of how your proposal will solve an important problem or bring new value to something. That end state should be motivating to the listener and build belief in your idea. Describing the current state of things and then describing your projected end state where the problem is solved by asking, "What if . . ." can be an effective technique. We made up the following example of this technique to illustrate the format:

> If you're like me, you have dozens of accounts on all kinds of apps and web-sites, and each of them has a login and password. All those credentials are constantly changing, different from one another, and impossible to remember. What if you could use just one set of credentials for any application, any time, and be totally secure? We are building that.

In the context of a job search, you won't quite be proposing anything (except that they hire you). Instead, an elevator pitch can be seen as a snap-shot of who you are, your goals, and what things might look like if you worked there. It can be a sentence or two about your main skills or value propositions, then a few ideas about what you would do if hired. The follow-ing is a hypothetical example of an elevator pitch you might have if, at the end of an interview, your interviewer takes you over to meet an executive and he asks what you would do at their company:

> I really want to work in marketing research, because I believe there is so much potential for behavioral science to better match consumers to products they really love. I would like to see all the types of data you collect and add some new variables to the mix. I think there is real opportunity to uncover some new ways to appeal to consumers.

It might be hard to propose a fully defined project, but a loose description of your ideas that feature your value proposition(s) can be useful to have on hand. As you become more familiar with the field that interests you, you can become more specific about ideas of what you will do once hired. It can be tricky to know just how specific to be, because in some positions or for some hiring managers, flexibility is required, and they might be turned off if they get the impression you have a set agenda—it might not fit what they need. For other positions, the hirer might have a well-defined role in mind for you (e.g., they need someone to transform their employee survey program). In those cases, specific actions would be appropriate to talk about (e.g., "I would learn from what you have now, analyze historic data for psychometric properties, match it to the literature, and gather information from stake-holders about what they want out of it"). Your standard go-to elevator pitch, however, should be generic and adaptable to any situation, and thus it might not include specific projects. If asked about a concrete role or project, as in the context of proposing a business, your pitch can certainly be specific.

Ideally an elevator pitch raises interest and causes the audience to ask you for more information (which you should also have ready). This is when you can refer to your other material—discussed in the rest of this chapter—or send a paper, résumé, or other items.

How to Craft an Elevator Pitch

- Find examples. Several outlets offer samples of elevator pitches.
  - An Internet search will yield a wealth of advice and examples. You can find examples both of business pitches and of advice on job seeker pitches.
  - A radio show segment by Carrie Feibel (2016) includes a discussion of graduate students practicing their pitches and has snippets of examples of quick elevator speeches that describe research.

- Start by describing your research. Write a simple 20- to 30-second description of your dissertation research or another project you have worked on. You can start with the practice writing you did for Chapter 5. At this point, do not worry about including an ask or proposal; simply take the work you did describing your research in a story form and craft it into a few short sentences that tell a compelling story. This exercise will help you get used to cutting some complicated ideas down to a few sentences that will generate interest from any reader or listener.

- Now try adding some future-state ideas. These can be career goals (refer to your mission and vision statements), general goals specific to a certain field, or even specific ideas for projects in your chosen field. If you are developing a business, write up your idea. The drafts that you generate now will be improved when you try them and get feedback and when you get to know more about the fields in which you would like to work. The present goal is to get accustomed to the format.

- Practice (and iterate!). Practice presenting your pitch, and pay attention to how it is received. Those statements or ideas that do not seem to generate much interest might be based in academic premises that are mismatched or unknown to your audience. Carefully think about each element of your pitch, and see if any are based on academic assumptions or values.

Venues for Practicing Your Elevator Pitch

Quite a few places near you likely offer guidance, advice, and practice for developing elevator pitches. For example, many local business incubators have sessions where entrepreneurs come and practice their pitches and get feedback from others. Attending these sessions as a spectator can be very helpful. You can find these organizations via an Internet search. They are often exclusive in the sense that you need to pay to use their resources or win a grant or a placement, but they sometimes host events that anyone can attend to work on skills or develop ideas. If you have a local incubator, watch for pitch practice sessions. Other leads may include the following:

- Small business support organizations. The U.S. Small Business Administration has a network of SBDCs that provide free or low-cost support to entrepreneurs and small businesses. They might host training or practice sessions for elevator pitches where you can find examples, and of course practice yours.

- Local chambers of commerce. Chambers also host events or networks that support small businesses. If these organizations do not host events near you, they will likely know if and where local events are held.

- Your graduate school or another school within the university. Many schools now have resources for undergraduate and graduate students to learn about and practice things such as elevator pitches. If you have such a resource at your school, we encourage you to take advantage of it.

- If your school does not already have a venue for practicing elevator pitches, we encourage you to organize one! You will probably find like-minded students from several disciplines who might be interested in practicing with a group. Ideally, you could even invite local entrepreneurs or members of the business or government community who could give feedback and advice or judge a competition.

LONGER DESCRIPTIVE PASSAGE

The next type of content you should be prepared to produce is a longer-form narrative. By now you can likely anticipate when this type of content could be useful—when you have the opportunity to speak for at least a few minutes or write for a few pages. It could be after you've presented your elevator speech and your audience invites you to say more. When you're sure you have someone's interest and they want to hear more, have a longer-form narrative ready to go.

For an entrepreneur, this might take the form of a written narrative on a business plan or proposal. It could also be in a conversation with a potential investor after your elevator pitch has successfully piqued interest. You can elaborate this longer-form passage any way that helps build interest and incorporates more of your talking points. When you are composing your one-sentence statement or elevator pitch, you have to drop many of your talking points. This longer passage is where you can add more of them in.

You could spend a little more time on the buildup, perhaps by providing additional research results to support the market need or potential customer base. You could also provide more details of your proposed product. No matter what the situation, if your talking points are well thought out and you have put the research and thinking into composing ways of speaking or writing about your proposed business or product, you can take full advantage of the opportunities you have to communicate with interested people.

In a job-seeking context, you could be asked to start off an interview by speaking for a few minutes. You can always feel out this kind of situation by beginning with your elevator speech; if the situation allows for more, you can elaborate using your longer written passage. You might also have several stages of an interview, and each new person you meet might ask you to start by saying a few things about yourself. Again, this is a great opportunity to mention more of your talking points. In short or unstructured conversation, you might not get the opportunity to hit many of them. When you get the chance to speak or write longer, do not hesitate to mention several. It is worth repeating that a recited list is not the ideal way to communicate in most contexts. This longer-form content should be strong and compelling but also a good fit for the context, and that will often call for a casual delivery, or at least a conversational tone that matches the mood and formality level of the audience.

Generally, the goal for this longer passage should be to memorably make a few points. It is not a good tactic to try to cram everything into a few dense sentences, the way you would with an abstract for a conference presentation or funding proposal. Instead, choose a few main ideas and thoroughly develop them. You can consider the situation, choose the top few talking points you think you should make, and work on those.

You should not expect anyone to remember more than a few main points from your narrative (with the exception of a hiring manager, who should be taking notes and likely following an interview guide). Most psychologists remember the seven plus-or-minus two rule for the number of ideas that can be held in one's working memory, but for busy professionals, seven *minus-four-or-five* is probably more realistic. Making a point more than once, or reinforcing a value proposition multiple times, can be very effective. For example, if one of your top talking points is that you can add expertise and perspective that a nonpsychologist cannot, you should mention that point early. Then you could briefly describe one of your lines of research and explain how that research would help you add your unique perspective to the work you would be doing.

To compose a longer descriptive passage, follow these steps:

1. Start with your messaging. Your messaging is a valuable list of strong points about your or your product's/business's potential value. A longer time to talk or space to write gives you a great opportunity to share these points.

2. Choose the points that are most important for your audience to remember. This could simply be the few talking points you've identified as the most important, or you could make a different choices for different contexts.

3. Next, compose the story or narrative you can tell to communicate those points. (By *compose*, we mean think about how you can play around with the points in different ways to form a narrative.) A recitation of points can be informative but is less compelling remarkable or memorable. A narrative, on the other hand, is easy to listen to and builds interest for the audience. Compose simple sentences that make clear points. Try both speaking and writing them.

4. Create different narratives for different audiences. A hiring manager, for example, probably has some specific expectations about certain details of your experience. A different person at the company could have an important voice in your hiring but might not have any specific expectations about your role or might not be familiar with your résumé. You might be better off highlighting points that you've found are memorable and impressive in those contexts. Similarly, if you are pursuing work in several different industries, the points you highlight or the story you tell about them might be different.

5. Try out your narratives on fellow students, friends, and family. Ask others to read them and give feedback. Revise accordingly—you can think you've crafted the most masterful way of describing a value proposition, but if no one else gets what you're trying to say, that's a good clue you might need to revise (or there might be a premise mismatch).

As we've recommended in every other chapter, be on the lookout for premises. If you have done so with your talking points, one-sentence statement, and elevator pitch, you will probably be in good shape at this point. But now that you are adding more material and telling more of a story, what you think is compelling might not be for others. For example, scientists are pretty excited by the inherent mystery in a research pursuit and the anticipation that builds when they finally have data cleaned and ready to analyze; the scientific process may be less exciting to someone outside the field. It will likely be necessary, then, to examine what you compose here once again.

This process of trial and error will likely never stop. As long as you need to communicate with others about your professional qualifications, it will be useful to keep your content sharp.

WRAP-UP

Your content and story particulars will be an evolving, changing bank of material. That will be truer the more you change jobs or the longer your search lasts. Spending time working on it now should be very helpful when you get into the thick of the search, or if your first job is more of a stepping-stone position to better-fitting jobs.

If you are planning for an academic career, then of course you are spending many hours preparing for it as you progress through your degree program. If you are interested in a nonacademic career, however, there is likely more that you will need to do to be successful. The work we discuss in this chapter can seem challenging and time-consuming—that's because it is. This is, however, the time for you to prepare for your career.

TAKEAWAYS

- It is important to develop content so you can have clear, compelling information on hand when you need it.

- Your messaging is a flexible set of talking points to which you can quickly refer in any casual or formal situation.

- A one-sentence statement, elevator pitch, and longer passage can be adapted to several types of situations in which you might find yourself during a career search.

WHAT TO DO NOW

Create a LinkedIn profile. LinkedIn is a social networking site that can be very important to a nonacademic career. Especially in your job search phase, your LinkedIn profile should be accurate, polished, and memorable. LinkedIn might be the first place that recruiters and hirers see you. Even after you land your first job, maintaining your profile can help you network inside your company and keep you visible outside your company in case the position turns out not to be the right fit.

Your profile should be genuine and accurate. There is no need to inflate your accomplishments or use some kind of corporate speak. Your photo should be clear and professional (unlike some other social network sites, this is not the place to use that selfie you took at the beach).

To get started, draft the content using the materials you developed in the previous chapters of this book. You should also consult other resources that can give you tips on how to use the various fields available; we recommend pieces by Amy George (2019) and Jon Shields (2018), but many more are available. For some fields, you can copy and paste directly from your résumé; other fields should have narrative content, which can be adapted from the content just described.

Next, show others your profile. You might look for certain types of feedback from certain audiences. Specifically, you might want to see if other psychologists feel that your content is contrived or trying too hard to fit into a different sector. From nonscientists, you might try to find out if your skills and value propositions are clear and understandable. If in the field(s) in which you want to work you have a network of professionals with whom you are close, you can even ask them to give you feedback on your profile. As with all your other content, we expect the process of perfecting your LinkedIn profile will be iterative and long-lasting. For example, if you shift from one job to another with a different focus, you might need to reframe your narrative content or the skills you highlight to tell the story of your career path.

PART IV

FINDING OR CHARTING THE PATH(S) AHEAD

Here we are. You have examined some of the premises you formed in your training as an academic psychologist, and you have reassessed your skills and experience in light of the values of a nonacademic workplace. You have drafted content and built materials for your job search. Are you ready to put it all to use?

In the next three chapters, we discuss several possible nonacademic career paths you are prepared for and might be interested in pursuing. You may have heard of some of these paths, or friends or classmates might have already taken them. Others paths you might never have considered. Regardless of which path you choose, you are well equipped to explore your options. With an open mind, you may very well discover the path that is just right for you.

9

WELL-WORN PATHS

In this chapter, we survey career paths that many PhDs, including psychologists, have followed. Because they are well-worn paths, many potential hirers for these careers will be familiar with academic credentials, and therefore they are not as fraught with premise-based challenges. Because these paths are well worn, they probably are familiar to many of your peers also. It is likely, therefore, that you will be competing against the same talent pool with whom you're competing for academic jobs. Some of the positions described in this chapter can pay very well, which makes them even more competitive. This is where your preparation could help set you apart from others; your ability to effectively communicate your value propositions and unique ideas should be an advantage. Perhaps more important, there are still a few subtle but foundational premise differences. Contract research organizations (CROs), and of course corporations, are businesses; their fundamental goals are financial. Government and grant agencies also have different operating models than an academic department. Your ability to show that you appreciate these differences, and your ability to shift away from some academic premises and toward the premises in these different worlds, could be very attractive to hirers. If a hirer has several equally

http://dx.doi.org/10.1037/0000170-011

The Portable PhD: Taking Your Psychology Career Beyond Academia, by P. Gallagher and A. Gallagher

qualified candidates for a position and one already shows the ability to adapt from a strictly academic mind-set to fit the needs of the organization, that is likely the candidate who will receive the offer.

This chapter introduces several career pathways and offers guidance on how to find and prepare for job opportunities. Much of the chapter, as well as the What to Do Now section, lays out activities to help you pursue these career paths. After you read this chapter, identify possible pathways you want to pursue, and consider some of the job options, Chapter 11 in this volume provides guidance on the next steps—actually applying for the jobs.

GRANTMAKING ORGANIZATIONS

Grantmaking agencies, which may operate in either the government or private sector, fund or otherwise support research. Many of these organizations both conduct research programs and fund other research projects, but some fund only outside research. Many of the positions in these organizations are administrative, which could include roles such as budget management, project planning and management, and report writing. You could, however, join a research team in some capacity and be responsible for certain aspects of the research process. It can feel disorienting at first to move away from conducting your own line of research, but many people find it rewarding to play a role in identifying research that could directly impact society.

An Internet search for *grantmaking agencies* will produce a listing of such agencies; listings can also be found at the U.S. Department of Health and Human Services (n.d.) site and in Urban and Linver's (2019) text. Similarly, a search for *private research foundations* or similar keywords will yield several listings of foundations. You can also find listings on the Social Psychology Network (n.d.) site, on the Candid website (www.foundationcenter.org), and in the Urban and Linver book. You may be familiar with the places in these lists as organizations to which you might apply for funding for your graduate research. The goal now, of course, is to visit different areas of the websites, or contact different people in the organizations, to look for potential employment.

How to Prepare and Search for a Granting Organization Job

The first and most obvious way to start your career search is to simply find job postings on websites. For positions at federal agencies, all positions are listed at the U.S. Office of Personnel Management website (https://

www.usajobs.gov). Many agencies, however, have their own sites for listings of their job openings (e.g., https://jobs.nih.gov/ for the National Institutes of Health), and some are not easy to find. For positions at private foundations or other organizations, the strategy is the same: visit websites and look for the pages on which job openings are listed.

If you are early enough in your graduate career that you do not need to start applying to jobs, you can start preparing for that eventuality by simply reading over these job listings. Reading through the open positions will start to give you an overview of the types of positions that are available at these organizations and the skills that are valuable to them. You can then purposively build experience in those areas during your graduate years. If you are later in your graduate career and ready to start applying for jobs, Chapter 11 of this volume presents guidance on the application process.

Next, seek opportunities to gain administrative experience. If your lab has grants, ask your advisor (or department business officer) to help you learn the process—not just the application process, but how to manage the grant once it's been awarded. There are likely accounting duties, reporting requirements, and scheduling that needs to be managed. Some labs might have a designated person (or people) to handle these duties. The more opportunities you have to learn all about the process and participate in it, the more you can include on your résumé.

If your lab does not have outside funding, find a lab in your department that does and ask if you can help there. You could volunteer to manage scheduling for a semester or a year or help analyze and plan the budget. A principal investigator (PI) and/or a member of a funded lab might be happy to have your help.

If you do not have any direct connections to opportunities like this, you can look for summer or part-time paid positions or internships at other labs. Many labs hire students or postdocs to do administrative tasks. There might be such a position, even if it is not in psychology, that could fit your schedule.

Finding Connections Inside Organizations

Another benefit of involving yourself with funded labs is that you can make connections at the funding agencies. Any lab with funding has necessarily interacted with individuals at the funding agency. Those people might be aware of open positions in their agency, and if they know you and know you are interested, they could put you in a good position to attract attention from the hirer. For example, there could be an administrative office at the agency or foundation that handles routine questions from research teams or helps with building grant applications. There might be one person with whom your research team regularly interacts—the main contact person at the funding organization. Alternatively, someone serving as a reviewer at the organization might be a friend or professional acquaintance of a researcher in your lab. You might find out about an opening, and even get your application noticed, by inquiring about open positions with that person.

It is important to keep in mind that you should pursue this type of inquiry only if the PI is comfortable with it. For a number of reasons, the PI might feel it is not appropriate to ask their contacts about possible job openings. We recommend that you discuss this strategy with your advisor or with the funded PI.

CONTRACT RESEARCH ORGANIZATIONS

Contract research organizations are companies set up to manage research for other organizations. Most are focused on the life sciences and specialize in carrying out clinical trials for pharmaceutical or medical device companies, but others have more specialized areas. Some include behavioral research, which might involve studying doctor or nurse behavior or patient experiences. For positions that are clearly psychology based, premises mismatches will likely be few—but again, your awareness of the differences between the academic and CRO contexts could be very valuable.

An Internet search for *contract research organizations* will yield several listings of these organizations. There are numerous CROs of all sizes and specialties. Some are likely near you. Many universities have affiliated CROs.

Because most CROs are focused on pharmaceuticals or medical devices, you might find that you need to explain why you, a behavioral scientist, would be interested in working at one. Keep in mind that smaller CROs are less likely to employ behavioral scientists. Depending on the type of position you are pursuing, you could refer to separate skill sets: For an administrative position, you could highlight your knowledge of the scientific method and any administrative experience. For a more research-focused position, you might need to explain what a behavioral scientist can add to studying products in the medical setting. For example, you could emphasize your work on cognitive processes involved in interacting with a digital display or the group dynamics processes in nursing teams that could affect usage. If you are applying for a position with an established behavioral science team, other candidates will probably have qualifications similar to yours. Here again, your ability to demonstrate your appreciation for and responsiveness to the premises differences might set you apart.

How to Prepare and Search for a CRO Job

Our guidance here is identical to the guidance we provided earlier for how to prepare for granting agency jobs. The principles are the same—read listings, gain administrative experience, and look for connections who work at CROs. A few possible wrinkles might be slightly different in the two searches, which we describe next.

You should have no trouble finding job listings on the websites of CROs. One difference, however, could be that CROs (especially larger ones) might have more robust HR departments and/or recruiters dedicated to the types of positions that interest you. That means there may be a recruiter with whom you can start a relationship. A recruiter is a company's HR person who helps hiring managers find candidates to fill positions. We discuss recruiters in more detail in Chapter 11.

Because contract research is such a big industry, you might also find placement or consulting companies that help connect candidates with positions at these companies. These services are essentially recruiter outsourcing: Companies engage them to help efficiently find talent to fill key positions. People from these agencies can be helpful contacts. Even if you do not fit a position to which you apply, getting your résumé on a list of candidates at one of these agencies might lead to other opportunities.

When you seek to gain administrative experience at a CRO, the most important difference you will note is that generally, federal (and even private) granting agencies operate on a fundamentally different model than a CRO, which is a business. Any experience you can gain in an administrative role at your academic institution will be helpful, but for a CRO position, it might be even more helpful if you can gain exposure to the concerns and pressures of a business. Accounting for the spending of grant dollars in your lab's operations and stretching funds to support more research activities is excellent experience, but working under an evolving operating budget or making a business case for reallocating funds are things that might set you apart at a CRO.

Business case. A *business case* is a rationale or justification for making a change or doing something new. A business case answers the question "Why should we do this?" It normally involves money—how much will the proposed action save, or how much more revenue will it generate? Sometimes it can be hard for a business or other organization to change course, get motivated to spend money on a new service, or invest in developing a new product. If a strong business case can be made, however, the organization is more likely to take action.

It might be challenging to find opportunities for this kind of experience within your lab or your department. Depending on the type of job you pursue, it might not be vital; many CROs who hire PhDs will be perfectly comfortable hiring researchers with no business experience, knowing that whatever acumen is necessary can be acquired on the job. However, if you are interested in business-related positions, or if you are eager to simply expand your skill set in the interest of differentiating yourself, one way to learn is to sit in on business classes at your school. Attending these classes—even undergraduate classes—could teach you basic terminology and/or current trends in the business world. Meeting professors or graduate students in the business school of your university or at other schools can also help. They are great resources for business-related knowledge, and you could even contribute by sharing knowledge about your training and the field of behavioral research.

Finding Connections Within a CRO

When you are looking to make connections, the main difference between granting organizations and CROs is the nature of relationships between professors and CROs. Professors have what amounts to partnerships with granting agencies. They are ongoing working relationships on specific projects. This type of partnership is much less likely with CROs; instead, people you know might know people who work for CROs. They might have been labmates in graduate school or other professional acquaintances who have found employment at a CRO. If your psychology department faculty do not know anyone who works at a CRO, faculty members in the life sciences departments might. You could approach friendly faculty in those areas and ask for their help in your career search.

THINK TANKS, NONPROFITS, AND PHILANTHROPY

Three other organization types that conduct research and regularly hire PhD researchers are think tanks, nonprofits, and philanthropic. The three typically have different missions or areas of focus, but their work can overlap, and they could offer similar positions for PhD psychologists. *Think tanks* are organizations set up to conduct research mainly focused on policy or government-related issues. Rand Corporation is one example; they conduct research related to, among other things, military matters. *Nonprofits* are charitable organizations, and they can have a wide range of missions. They often focus on social issues such as education or homelessness. Nonprofits can be considered *philanthropic* organizations, which (as the name indicates) are set up to benefit a cause or a group of people.

Generally, you can find administrative or research roles with these organizations that are similar to positions at grantmaking agencies or foundations or at CROs. Administrative positions could include managing projects, reviewing funding applications, or administering funds, and research positions could range from specific roles in larger research lines to consulting on several projects. Think tanks are likely to have the most robust and well-established research programs, and research-focused positions can be expected to be highly competitive. Nonprofits and philanthropic organizations might not have large research areas.

You can find listings of these organizations with Internet searches. There are also centralized resources for them; for example, The Chronicle of Philanthropy site (https://www.philanthropy.com) has job listings, as does National Nonprofits (https://nationalnonprofits.org).

INDUSTRIAL/ORGANIZATIONAL POSITIONS

For psychologists trained in research-focused subfields, industrial/organizational (I/O) psychology can be a complete mystery. If your department does not have an I/O area, you might never be exposed to what an I/O psychologist studies or does. Perhaps the most fundamental difference between training in I/O psychology compared with research-centered training is that I/O psychologists are trained both as researchers and practitioners. I/O psychology programs regularly place PhDs in nonacademic jobs and are therefore plugged into many career paths that might be possibilities for other psychologists.

Many I/O psychologists go into HR jobs, which might include several functions such as measuring employee engagement, training, assessing job candidates' personality, analyzing jobs, or advising organizational change projects. These roles and the other functions that I/O psychologists perform could be done by, or informed by, psychologists from other subfields.

Many organizations that hire I/O psychologists are perfectly familiar with the training an I/O psychologist receives but may not understand the difference between I/O psychologists and those with different types of training. The biggest challenge in this scenario will likely be to explain why you—especially if you have no formal training in a business or other setting—would be a better hire than an I/O psychologist.

How might you answer the question of why you're a better candidate than an I/O psychologist? For a research-focused position, you might highlight that you had more research training and experience than is typically offered in an I/O graduate program and talk about the research projects you led and published. For a nonresearch position, it might be more helpful to highlight that you have likely had more extensive and deep training in theory, which gives you more creative insights into the job's main focus areas. For a more expert hirer, you could even talk about the specific theories or schools of thought you studied and explain why that training could add unique value to the position. As you learn about the I/O field and start talking to connections or potential hirers about possible jobs, you will be able to build your own case for your advantages.

To search for and prepare for an I/O job, first learn about I/O psychology. If you are an experimental psychologist pursuing work in a field in which I/O psychologists work, it is crucial to understand how I/O psychologists are trained, what they typically do on the job, and what kind of qualifications they normally have. One way to learn this is to read an introductory or graduate-level I/O survey textbook. Another way is to sit in on introductory or higher level I/O classes if possible. A third way is to read the Society for Industrial and Organizational Psychology (SIOP) website (https://www.siop.org) and review the resources it offers. This site can give you an overview of the issues that I/O psychologists study and the state of the field. Its jobs page lists openings, which can give a clear picture of the types of positions I/O psychologists can fill. Finally, follow SIOP on social media (especially LinkedIn and Twitter). This is a great way to discover what I/O psychologists are thinking about and the topics they see as important. Having a familiarity with the issues of the day could show hirers that you are informed about the field and make them more confident that you could learn anything an I/O PhD might know and you do not already know.

Next, find job listing outlets and build your network. Learning about the I/O psychology field should also show you many avenues to pursue in order to find jobs. The SIOP job listing page is just one resource. Interacting with I/O psychologists will likely expose you to other ways they search for and find jobs. Of course, this could be a great way to expand your professional network. I/O professors and graduate students likely have many colleagues who work in industry or government settings.

WRAP-UP

In this chapter, we covered four general nonacademic areas in which psychologists have often found work. These career paths are "well worn" in the sense that many psychologists like you have followed them. Some of them might be unfamiliar to you, and some hirers might not be accustomed to seeing candidates with your particular training, but premise mismatches and obfuscations should not be as much of a problem here as they might be on other career paths.

We hope this brief overview of these possible paths makes you optimistic about the nonacademic opportunities that might be out there for you. These are certainly not the only paths—read on for more ideas!

TAKEAWAYS

- Working in grantmaking organizations, CROs, nonprofits, or positions normally filled by I/O psychologists are four established career pathways for psychologists.

- Reading job listings, gaining administrative experience, and networking can be effective ways to pursue these career paths.

- Learning more about I/O psychology can open unseen career options and can be good preparation for the job market.

WHAT TO DO NOW

Using the websites cited in this chapter, explore job listings in the four main areas that were listed. If one area interests you more than others, find more than one listing. Even if you do not feel qualified for the position, study the listing.

Now think about how you might seek to build your professional network in ways that might help you get these types of jobs. Generate a list of ways you could build your network. Is there a mailing list you could subscribe to? A conference or local meetup you could attend? A conversation you could open with someone whose connections might lead you to employers in this area? There might be several degrees of separation between you and someone who might connect you with this hirer, so be creative. What conference or event could you attend (preferably one that includes a networking event or workshop) where you might meet someone who could introduce you to another field? What department or area of the organization does each position sit in? What other kind of work might be done in that department?

After generating your list of ideas, act on them. Which ones seem most promising? It might take considerable time for a network to bear fruit, so do not pass judgment too quickly. The key is to maintain contact and periodically check in with people in your network.

10 LESS WORN PATHS

The careers covered in Chapter 9 of this volume are in organizations that often are heavily connected to academia. The goals and operating models of those organizations are different from academic departments, but the familiarity with academia makes transitioning to those careers easier.

In this chapter, we turn to career paths that are considerably different from academia. It is not unprecedented for psychologists to go into these careers, but the pathways to them are not well worn, so premises differences can be a larger issue. Many hirers will be only vaguely familiar with the value a psychologist can add to their field, and most graduate psychology programs provide no guidance for learning about or pursuing careers in these fields.

For each career path we describe in this chapter, we list several job titles or keywords you can use to search for job listings. You can use these as starting points for the searching process we describe in Chapter 11.

For the fields we present here, we try to use the most common terms and titles we have encountered, but there might be variations depending on the specific company or subfield. We point this out not just as a disclaimer for

http://dx.doi.org/10.1037/0000170-012
The Portable PhD: Taking Your Psychology Career Beyond Academia, by P. Gallagher and A. Gallagher

ourselves—it raises an important point. One way to demonstrate to a skeptical interviewer that you are familiar with a field is to demonstrate facility with some of the variations in terminology between subfields or industry leaders. It is advantageous to attend to and take notes about the variations you come across in job listings, conversations, and other materials in a field you are exploring. One PhD psychologist who works in business told us, "I would learn the baseline terminology when applying. For example, when I applied to a bank, I learned all of the key words around option trading to appear more knowledgeable in the interview."

MARKETING AND MARKET RESEARCH

The field of marketing has a history of being a destination for psychologists. Nevertheless, this field has its own training programs and professional organizations, and it grants its own degrees (undergraduate and graduate). Most of the marketing workforce are not psychologists, and therefore they can subscribe to quite different premises.

The good news is that marketing includes many roles that psychologists can fill. You could specialize in one of the roles listed here or, more likely, experience several of them in one job.

Market research is an umbrella term that can cover multiple role types. One thing market researchers (or analysts) do is study a market. A marketplace can be an actual geographical area such as a city or simply the supply of and demand for a product type. Sample goals of market analysis could be to understand the competition, identify the best location for a new store, or identify a need that current products are not filling. This type of research does not focus on individual consumers per se. A social scientist can contribute to this work by designing studies, analyzing data, or synthesizing conclusions—essentially as a methodologist. Content knowledge of psychology can certainly help as well. For example, a social psychologist might contribute valuable insights into social forces that shape attitudes or demand in marketplaces.

Market research (or marketing research) can also refer to studying consumers—topics such as people's attitudes toward a product, their likelihood to buy under certain circumstances, or their impressions of brands or companies. These topics are direct applications of psychological science, so it is clear how a psychologist can add value in these positions. Some positions might call for a technical methodologist, but others can be a position in which a psychologist can add valuable ideas about what to measure, how to measure it, and how to use findings to shape communications or products.

In both types of marketing research, psychologists can often contribute novel theoretical insights or ideas. For example, many psychologists are familiar with theories of persuasion, motivation, or decision making that are often not part of marketing training.

Titles or keywords: market analyst, market research analyst, market research, analyst, marketing manager.

PUBLIC RELATIONS

Public relations (or PR) is sometimes considered an area of marketing. It is also an area of communications. It is distinct from marketing in that is it focused on the relationship between an entity and its consumer base, its supporters, or the general public, and it normally focuses on a different set of channels or communication contexts (e.g., a PR office works with speeches or public appearances by a CEO, press releases, or a political candidate's campaign talking points; marketing works more with advertising materials or product packaging).

There is something of a debate in the PR industry and among its customers about whether and how PR and its effects can be measured. Psychologists can potentially contribute a great deal toward answering those questions. One of our favorite things about being research psychologists is figuring out how to measure those "soft" variables that seem so hard to quantify. Psychologists' experience with that particular challenge could help a PR firm learn what practices work better and under what conditions. Like in other areas, psychologists could also contribute original ideas that veterans of the industry might not see—for example, novel ideas about the psychological mechanisms that could affect how the public processes certain messages or events.

In any role in a marketing department or company, you could contribute in several ways. You could serve as a research methodology expert, as a human behavior expert, or both. You could even specialize in data analysis; many psychologists have advanced quantitative skills that professionals from other backgrounds have not had as much opportunity to exercise. You could have an internal consulting role, in which different teams from around the department or company come to you for guidance or ideas, or you could play a set role on a team.

Titles or keywords: PR manager, communications, branding, brand manager.

PRODUCT DEVELOPMENT

An area closely related to marketing is product development. As briefly defined earlier, *product development* is the process of designing and building offerings that a company can sell. After reading Chapter 6 of this volume, you have a good idea of the components of product development and how a psychologist can contribute. We build on that discussion here.

Companies have had research and development (R&D) departments for years, where product development takes place. An appliance company, for example, might think of a new design for a refrigerator, refine the technology so the parts can be affordably mass-produced, and test how consumers react, all in the R&D department. Larger corporations are likely to invest more in this area, although many smaller companies often have some product development work in progress. In fact, many startups are essentially developing a product or products as their main activity.

Psychologists can contribute to product development in much the same way as they can contribute to marketing or other functions. Research methodology expertise can be valuable when testing different variations of a new feature or product, or for any kind of pilot-testing or trial and error development. Statistical acumen is especially valuable here as well. For example, multiple variations of a software product or feature might be tested in different subgroups of consumers over time, creating rich data sets that need to be carefully analyzed. A psychologist can also be valuable in testing consumer reaction to products because attitudes, impressions, and judgments are the primary outcome variables in that research. Content expertise can also be extremely valuable: Psychologists can help gather insights into consumers' needs (which might be considered a market research function) and then help a product development team figure out how to design products to address those needs. This is perhaps another underappreciated potential role of psychologists: They can offer novel predictions about how a certain product or feature would or would not meet consumer needs.

One parallel career path to a product development position in a company is a product development consultant. Such a consultant contributes the same types of skills or theoretical expertise as just described but is hired to work on defined projects. You could get into this career by finding projects in an internship capacity (paid or unpaid) and trying to parlay that experience into another gig until you can build a reputation and client base (this could take several years—we discuss consulting as a career next). Another way to build this career would be to get a position in product development; build experience there; and then, when you feel you might have clients that would be willing to hire you independently, pursue independent work.

Titles or keywords: Product development is such a well-defined occupation that searching the words *product development jobs* will yield the most relevant listings.

USER EXPERIENCE

User experience (UX) is how a consumer or user interacts with a product or environment. It normally refers exclusively to digital products and environments. You might think of UX as the digital equivalent of ergonomics (although some might not make that distinction, perhaps treating UX as a larger umbrella term). Working in UX, you might analyze users' attitudes toward a newly redesigned website, survey users on their opinions of the aesthetic appeal of a site, or measure how much faster users can navigate a new game's architecture.

In its simplest form, UX can address whether a product is usable. Can users accomplish what they need to? Does everything work as it should? In more complex UX analyses, eye movements, response times, or implicit attitudes might be measured to compare two or more competing designs. It is easy to see how a research psychologist could contribute to those efforts—many of us have spent hundreds of hours in psychology lab rooms programming and conducting studies just like these!

When searching for UX careers, you will likely come across listings for jobs in *user interface* (UI) as well. A listing might have both (e.g., UI/UX Designer). UI is closely related to UX, and we suspect that many positions blend the two roles. In some companies, however, there might be important distinctions between the types of backgrounds they seek in job candidates for these two roles—for example, a psychologist might be very well suited for a UX role, but a UI role might require graphic design background. If you are interested in pursuing this career, learning more about the distinctions between these roles would be a great way to prepare.

Once again, we feel that in UX, as in many other fields, psychologists can contribute as highly skilled research design and methodology experts and/or as content experts. Clearly, many cognitive psychologists could contribute to a UX effort as expert methodologists, but they and psychologists from other subfields could also generate novel psychological variables to measure in the area of UX that could add value that many companies are not currently realizing.

Titles or keywords (for any of the following, *user interface* can replace *user experience*): user experience designer, user experience researcher, user experience consultant, user experience analyst.

QUANTITATIVE ANALYSIS, DATA SCIENCE, AND RELATED FIELDS

The "big data" craze of a few years ago resulted in a lot of companies, big and small, recording tons of data on all aspects of their operations, their employees, and their consumers. Many companies quickly realized that they lacked the ability to extract the value out of those giant data sets that they were anticipating. How should those data be analyzed? What modeling techniques are appropriate? What questions can these data help answer?

If quant is your main area in psychology, if you consider yourself a hacker, or even if you just took extra stats classes and actually liked the data analysis parts of your research projects, those skills and interests could be the basis of a career path. Numerous smaller companies have data they don't know how best to utilize, and bigger companies with quant teams are often hiring.

Many quant-oriented jobs are specialized to their industry. For instance, quant positions at financial institutions often require expertise in finance-related quant techniques (e.g., procedures used in stress testing). You might be competing with accounting, economics, or computer science PhDs. Very likely, you will see many data scientists, a relatively recent title that refers (broadly) to people who manage and/or analyze data. Data scientists are in high demand because they are highly skilled and ostensibly can get value out of the mountains of data that organizations collect. Data scientists, however, often do not have training in psychology, or indeed in any behavioral theory. For this reason, your psychology training could be a strong differentiator for you.

Many universities and other institutions now provide training in data science. This would be a great addition to your experience in graduate school. If you do not have the most competitive coding experience, software expertise, or facility with specific statistical methods, a program in data science could shore up those skills. That, combined with your training in human behavior, could make you especially competitive for the growing number of data-centered jobs. For a smaller company just building up an analysis function, you might be a perfect fit.

Perhaps the most promising subfield in this area for research psychologists is *people analytics,* which is, essentially, analyzing HR data for useful insights. This is a relatively recent movement to learn more from the data that most companies collect about their people—tenure, performance evaluations, promotions, and information such as engagement levels or other survey responses. Analyzing those data can potentially reveal new insights into important outcomes such as propensity to quit, the best timing for promotions, or employee needs that managers should address. A research psychologist is an ideal fit for a position in this area, for both research/ statistical skill and content expertise.

Titles or keywords: analyst, quantitative analyst, people analytics/analyst, human resources analyst, quant technology, research, models or modeling.

CONSULTING

Plenty of psychologists have found their way into careers in consulting, but most studied counseling, industrial/organizational (I/O), or even clinical psychology. We suspect the number of research-focused PhDs in consulting is much smaller. Consulting is, like the other fields described in this chapter, something for which most research psychologists receive no training or orientation.

A job in consulting can take many forms. A giant global consulting firm (e.g., McKinsey, Bain, Gallup) will have many defined roles and well-developed career tracks that new hires will normally follow. Such firms have likely hired many research psychologists (and for that matter, people with myriad qualifications) and will have a procedure for helping new hires build any skills they lack. They will also already have ideas for the roles a psychologist might play.

Smaller consulting firms, on the other hand, might not have any behavioral scientists and might not understand the potential value of hiring you. They should be intrigued by what you could bring, however (if a company has shown interest, you can assume they are), and be interested in hearing your pitch. In this situation, keep in mind that part of the value that a consulting firm offers its clients is the unique qualifications of its consultants. Therefore, when a consulting firm interviews you for a possible position, the more you can help them envision "selling" your qualifications to potential clients, the better. You might even ask an interviewer what their clients are looking for or asking about and then describe (as best you can) how you can meet those needs. If your interviewer can envision adding your skills to what they pitch to prospects, they will be more likely to be excited about hiring you.

Some companies that are not consulting firms have positions with the word *consultant* in the job title. The consultant title likely refers to the role the position plays in the company; it is probably a position that provides a service to other teams or individuals across the company on an as-needed basis. These positions often have well-defined duties to perform, which is different from what you might find at a consulting firm, where your duties could be more varied and change over time.

Consulting positions can include an wide array of tasks and duties. You could focus mainly on supporting functions, such as research or program evaluation, or you could act in client-facing functions, actually delivering programs or services to clients. A research role at a consulting firm might include original laboratory or field research, in which you try to generate new knowledge about the company's field of expertise. It might also include analyzing markets or analysis of clients' data for new insights. Program evaluation is measuring the effects of training or interventions. Many developmental psychologists are familiar with measuring the effects of school or early childhood interventions, and psychologists who have worked in behavioral health are likely familiar with measuring outcomes of health interventions. These are strong qualifications to go into program evaluation in a consulting firm (or other companies).

Another consulting firm position could be product development. Instead of software or actual material products, consulting firms develop programs, training, or interventions as their products. How these products are designed, tested, and improved can follow largely the same steps as any other product, and a research psychologist can be well qualified to do this work.

Finally, the type of position that most people probably think of when they hear the word *consultant* is a client-facing position. People in these positions deliver the products or services to the client—they are the face and voice of the firm. Most firms will have well-defined products or approaches that they will expect you to deliver, but most will also support your developing your own persona or approach. As just mentioned, a consulting firm will often be interested in selling not only their particular brand of materials but also their personnel. A large well-known firm might be more focused on delivering firmly established, consistent products, whereas a smaller firm might do more to feature you individually as the "product." (It will be in your best interest to figure out where on this spectrum a potential employer lands so you can best understand what they are looking for.) In some positions, you might start by focusing on support functions while your client-facing skills are assessed or developed, and then move into client-facing roles later.

Client-facing. *Client-facing,* or customer-facing, refers to a job function that includes face-to-face interaction with the client. In contrast, non-client-facing roles might be called support or back-office roles. For example, a salesperson in a clothing store would be customer-facing, and an HR employee at the company's main office would be in a non-client-facing role. Many companies have special training for client-facing roles, and client skills are often a distinct set of qualifications for which you will be evaluated or trained.

Another career that might interest you is an independent consultant. On this career path, you would work individually with clients offering any service you can. A sustainable independent consultant career can take years to build as you gather a client base and hone your offerings. We discuss this path further next.

Titles and search terms: Any form of the word *consultant*, program evaluation, research, human resources consultant, executive coaching, team building, employee engagement, analyst.

GOVERNMENT/MILITARY

Federal, state, and local governments are among the largest employers in the United States, and as such they comprise many different jobs. Many agencies, including the military, regularly hire psychologists, mainly in clinical or counseling roles but also in research-oriented roles. A behavioral scientist might contribute to behavioral health research in VA research centers or conduct research within the military or in other government agencies. Much of this research might be similar to research conducted in business settings—improving HR operations, maximizing employee engagement, optimizing operating efficiency, or similar projects.

The central listing website for all federal government positions is with the U.S. Office of Personnel Management (https://www.usajobs.gov). We recommend including this site in your job search process. If you are interested in state and local positions, simply search state and local government websites for their listings to learn what positions might be a fit for you. Becoming acquainted with different government positions and talking with potential hirers could make you more competitive for these positions.

Titles or search terms: We have found that federal jobs for which psychologists are qualified normally include the word *psychologist* in the title. The U.S. Office of Personnel Management website (https://www.usajobs.gov) also lists job titles and occupations that include a search term, so searching terms like *psychologist*, *research*, and *analyst* could uncover positions that might be interesting.

ENTREPRENEURSHIP

By *entrepreneurship*, we mean starting up and establishing a working business. This could include a not-for-profit organization, but most frequently it takes the form of starting a for-profit business.

Starting up a business includes various stages and tasks. You need an idea, a way to make that idea profitable, a detailed plan for how you will proceed, and (probably) partners to help you carry out and/or fund that plan. You became familiar with business plans in Chapter 4 and with marketing and product development in Chapters 6 through 8 of this volume. All of these functions are involved in starting a business.

A major component for most entrepreneurs is obtaining funding. Most individuals do not have tens of thousands of dollars lying around to fund a startup, so they need to convince investors to "bet" on their idea by investing money. As you can imagine, this process is highly competitive. Most funders have specific requirements to be met before they consider investing, and much of the entrepreneurship process is dedicated to meeting those requirements.

Alternatively, you could "bootstrap" your business, which means to start at a small scale that does not require big initial money and fund your expansion with revenue generated by the business itself. The downside of this process is that it can take a very long time. Your circumstances and your preferences should shape the path you choose. If you have the time to build a business slowly and do not want to compete for funding or share your ownership, bootstrapping might be the method for you.

Individual entrepreneurs can play different roles in these ventures. You could be a one-person team, performing every role and doing every task yourself. You could also specialize in one or more roles (e.g., designing marketing plans) and then join several teams, each working on startup projects. It is not uncommon for entrepreneurs to be involved in several projects concurrently. If you become part of the local entrepreneurship community and demonstrate a strength in some area, you might be recruited to join other teams in return for a stake in future profits.

Unlike how psychologists might be viewed in other career fields that we discuss in this chapter, a psychologist in entrepreneurship might not raise eyebrows at all. People in this career pursuit come from all kinds of backgrounds, including academic. In fact, many business incubators are affiliated with universities and are designed to help "productize" scientific discoveries or inventions of their faculty. Most such incubators have been built around tried-and-true lines of business such as medical devices and pharmaceuticals, and they might not immediately see how to productize findings from a psychology lab, so in that sense you might need to rely on some compelling communication of your skills and value propositions. In the general entrepreneurship scene, however, our experience is that behavioral scientists are met with curiosity, interest, and welcome.

As we have already implied, a research psychologist could play many roles in the entrepreneurship process. You could specialize in a role that psychologists are already well qualified to perform, such as market analysis, or you could find that you like to build business plans and contact investors. You might also start something completely on your own, perhaps even as a side project, and build it slowly over time. Many entrepreneurs do just this. Your new familiarity with the topics we have covered in this book should help you find the types of work that attract you, and if you do pursue entrepreneurship in some form, you can do so in a way that best fits your career goals.

Titles and search terms: As you might expect, there are few listings for "entrepreneurs" on job boards! However, local startup communities or similar groups might have a forum where teams list their needs. For example, your local chamber of commerce might have an entrepreneur group with which a team that needs marketing help might advertise. We refer you to the second What to Do Now activity in Chapter 4 to explore where you might find these local groups.

WRAP-UP

Psychologists can successfully pursue nontraditional careers. You might even know of someone who left your lab years ago to work in a mysterious job in marketing or product research. Your graduate program, however, probably offers no training in, or even introduction to, these alternate career paths or in how to prepare for them.

In this chapter, we introduced many of those careers and tried to clear just a bit of the mystery around them. With these quick introductions to alternative careers, we hope you can set off exploring some new possibilities for yourself.

TAKEAWAYS

- Certain nonacademic careers can be quite open to research psychologists, but most are not addressed in your graduate training.

- Use the brief introductions in this chapter to start thinking about possible paths. Then continue your own exploration of paths that pique your interests.

- Finding your own path can be an unpredictable but fulfilling journey that ends in a career that fits your priorities and desired lifestyle.

WHAT TO DO NOW

Choose one of the areas listed earlier in this chapter, and learn enough about it such that you can speak credibly about how you could add value in it. If one of the areas seems interesting as a career path, you should certainly start to learn more about it. This activity might be most enlightening, however, if you choose an area that does not actually seem very interesting to you now.

In any of the areas, there are perhaps dozens of positions to work in. For example, in the broad field of UX, there are UI engineers and designers, UX researchers, content strategists, web analytics experts, and more. The goal of this activity is to learn about those different positions and the roles they would play in a company, in an independent consultant capacity, in a government agency, or anywhere else, and then to learn enough about the field and at least one job title to identify how a research psychologist could be valuable.

Simple searches for job titles using the keywords presented earlier should uncover related keywords and sources of information that explain what the field is and does, the different types of jobs it offers, the expected education of applicants, and the history of the field. Various websites and books provide guidance in the fields, definitions of industry-specific vocabulary terms, explanations of different job roles, and more.

Learn about each of several job types within each field, and pay attention to things such as how the field evolved or central theories or models. Try to avoid focusing too much on one job type, because you might miss other lines of investigation. Once you feel you have learned the basics, dig in deeper and find more information until you can imagine having an informed conversation with a professional in the field. (And of course, if you become interested in a possible career, start having those conversations by reaching out to recruiters, applying for jobs, or attending local meetups or conferences!)

If you do this exercise, you will gain practice in investigating an unfamiliar career and learning enough about it to make a credible case for how a psychologist could add value. If you successfully explore one career, you will be able to do this same process for other career paths and thus expand your field of possibilities. This process could start to build a habit of such investigations, so you will begin to see prospects for careers you had never considered. Ideally, if you do this regularly, you will generate a long list of new paths to investigate.

11 HOW TO APPLY FOR JOBS

In this chapter, we describe an approach to applying for jobs that goes beyond simply crafting résumés and submitting them. Our suggested approach will help you match your skills to the job market. It can be applied to any job search in any field. We provide the actual steps you can follow to start your search, with special attention to learning what doctoral-level psychologists are not routinely taught in their graduate training. If you find other resources that give you helpful advice, you should absolutely use them as well!

Of course, if your main goal is to start up a business, there are no job listings for that. Applying for jobs, however, can lead to your finding employment while you are building your business, which can be significant in helping you learn about the industry you want to join.

We list the activities in this chapter as a series of steps. This format makes it easier to describe the details and value of each activity, and in the beginning, going step by step makes it easier to manage all these activities. Once you start, however, you will most likely find yourself taking many of these steps at the same time. Once you talk to recruiters or hirers (Step 5), for example, you will learn more about how to read job listings (Step 2) and tweak your résumé (Step 3).

http://dx.doi.org/10.1037/0000170-013
The Portable PhD: Taking Your Psychology Career Beyond Academia, by P. Gallagher and A. Gallagher

STEP 1: PREPARE TO ITERATE

Applying to jobs is a lengthy process. You will probably experience many starts and stops. In many ways, it is even more unpredictable than the academic market, in which you send out a batch of application packages at a set time of year, proceed through a predictable pattern of next steps, then start again the next year (if you didn't land a job). Each application in the nonacademic world is its own thread, and those threads can run their own unique course for months, a year, or longer before you gain traction and land a job.

You should expect to submit many applications that do not lead to a callback or an interview, and that is perfectly fine. It is hard to know how to stand out in the world of electronic application materials and automated screening tools. Submitting applications to listings is just one of the strategies you can use to pursue jobs, so it might not be the strategy that directly results in a career. But it is certainly important to do, and even the applications you submit that do not land you a job can provide valuable information about the job possibilities that are out there and how you can successfully pursue them.

One way to prepare for a potentially long and sometimes frustrating job search is with deep self-reflection. The previous chapters of this book and their What to Do Now activities should have spurred the kind of reflection we refer to. The goal of the self-reflection is to think about what you value in a career, what you would be happy or unhappy with in your work, what kind of compensation you would accept, and similar goals. Establishing these parameters, and being explicit about your values, can provide guidance and even peace of mind during your search (much as a personal vision or mission statement might).

STEP 2: READ JOB LISTINGS

Now that you have braced yourself for the potentially long process of applying, it is time to start exploring what's out there. Reading job listings informs you of the range of possible jobs in a particular area and might open your eyes to jobs you had not considered before. The chief value of reading job listings, at least in the beginning of your search, is to identify what skills are sought after for the jobs you want and how those skills are described in the industry in which you want to work.

You can find listings by simply searching any of the major job listings sites (Indeed.com, Monster.com, LinkedIn.com, and CareerBuilder.com are just a few) or searching online for jobs in the area you are pursuing (e.g., "market research jobs"). Job listings might also appear in other sources outside of a general Internet search—sources such as professional society pages, subscription email lists, and trade publications. Listings—even unlisted job openings—can also come from people in your professional network. As mentioned earlier in this book, networking is a great source for information about how to frame your skills; it can also be how you find out about new openings. The more you look and the more you make connections, the more sources you will find for job listings.

Reading job listings might be a bit more challenging than it sounds. For example, you might be interested in a user experience position, so you begin reading those listings. The job descriptions and required skills might be completely unintelligible. If this happens, you need to learn more about the industry or field. You can take the required skills listed in those job postings, search them online, read about what they mean, and try matching your skills to them. Even if the job descriptions and required skills do make sense, what the job poster means by "research" might be different from your working definition. To adjust for this, you should read job listings from several companies—or, if possible, several types of industries—and note if and how they describe their jobs differently. Are the variations just idiosyncratic company lingo? Are there commonalities in the descriptions that you see used across the field?

The goal is, of course, to learn as much as you can about the desired skills and abilities in your target field. This process—reading and researching actual job listings and the skills and abilities they seek—is how a lot of the mystery about nonacademic jobs can start to clear up. In your graduate studies you have probably never been trained to understand the skills, for example, a consulting company looks for. As a result, a business consulting career might sound very interesting, but you likely have no idea how to describe or develop the necessary skills. Taking the step of applying for a few jobs can begin to clarify that mystery into concrete actions you can take. Following the next steps we describe can fill in the rest of the missing knowledge.

STEP 3: POST RÉSUMÉS

Step 3 is uploading résumés and profiles to job sites. This is separate from actually applying to jobs—instead, you create an account and a profile on each site. When you create a profile and upload your résumé, the site will give you customized job listings based on the keywords you included.

As you read and analyze these filtered listings, you'll learn more about how your résumé looks out in the market and the types of jobs that the automatic algorithms in the job sites match to you.

This task might appear to be quite difficult because the number of suggested jobs might be overwhelming or the jobs might not make sense to you. Don't despair. You will make this task of sorting through suggested jobs and identifying promising ones more manageable as you continue to follow the upcoming steps.

Don't worry about posting the perfect résumé right now. That would be nearly impossible until you know much more about the industry and jobs you're targeting. Expect to revise your résumé several times as you refine your knowledge about special terms and skills.

In fact, systematically varying your résumé is the next stage we recommend. It is a great way to start sorting through the myriad jobs suggested to you by these sites. Making changes, and then examining the differences in suggested jobs that result, can help you understand what certain job titles or required skills mean in different industries. For example, you could create one résumé that highlights one of your interests (say, project management), upload it, and read through the suggested jobs that result. Then you could create and upload a different résumé that features another interest, like research methodology; post it a few weeks later; and examine the differences in suggested jobs. Through this process you can start to learn where your skills might be more valued, or which career path might be more promising. At the very least, this step can help you start making more sense of the job postings you see.

STEP 4: APPLY TO JOBS

After studying the landscape of job possibilities, the next step is to start applying. Once you have explored the types of jobs that interest you, and learned the terminology associated with them, we encourage you to start submitting applications.

Even if you are not yet finished with your PhD training, and even if you are not sure you would take a job if it were offered, it is advisable to start submitting applications. You need to start to learn how to attract the attention of potential hirers and convince them of your value, and this step is where that happens. We are not suggesting you submit applications to everything you see, but if a job looks as if it could fit, you should apply. You can be perfectly honest at all stages of the process—for example, if you apply to a job you probably would not take and the hirer contacts you, you can make your conditions clear. What would it really take for you to consider the job? For example, you might explain that you couldn't start until after you defend your dissertation, you would require a salary of $150,000 a year, and you would need your moving expenses covered. If the hirer is still interested, then you might be too!

As we already stated, you should expect that most of the applications you submit will not result in a callback or other response. Don't feel rejected— there are many reasons why your application wouldn't be considered that have nothing to do with your personal merit.

It is important to recognize that the job offers you do not receive can still yield valuable information. To illustrate, imagine you apply to several researcher positions with no success, but your applications to administrative positions generate some interest (e.g., a phone screen, an email inquiry from the hirer). In this case, your credentials for administrative positions are more attractive to hirers, which might lead you to either revise your researcher-geared materials to catch more attention or apply to more administrative positions based on the conversations you have with potential hirers.

In sum, applying to jobs, even if you likely would not accept their offers, can result in valuable feedback that you can apply to your search. Most applications will likely go nowhere. From some you might receive a soulless rejection form letter. However, one or two applications might bring you an email or call. Any conversation you have with someone interested in your application will likely be informative about what they are looking for and if they understand how you describe what you can do. Talking to people is the subject of the next step.

STEP 5: CONTACT RECRUITERS AND HIRERS

Recruiters and hirers are two of the best sources of information on how to translate your skills to nonacademic jobs. These people are doing the work of matching candidates with jobs and hiring them. Information from them can provide answers that you haven't found elsewhere.

Recruiters can be either representatives of one company ("in-house" recruiters) or independent, providing services to multiple client companies. Their work in both cases is to find promising candidates for jobs and bring them to the hirer. (We use the generic term *hirer* here to refer to the person who actually has the opening on their team that they need to fill. This role is often called the *hiring manager*.) Some hirers will not have the services of a recruiter and will be conducting the job search on their own. Hirers will have all the details about their specific job, whereas recruiters will be familiar with a wider range of jobs and potential openings. Both the recruiter and the hirer will have valuable information—namely, the knowledge of what characteristics, skills, or talents the "promising" candidate possesses.

We recommend never passing up an opportunity to talk with a recruiter or hirer, because each conversation you have is an opportunity to learn. A potential hirer could call and discover after talking with you a few minutes that your qualifications are not a match for the job. You might even already know you're not likely to be a good match. You could still take the call, however, and be prepared to ask about other positions at the organization, ask if the person is aware of other jobs that your qualifications might match, or ask about the skills that would make you a match for this or other jobs. The hirer might know of another opening that is a better fit or remember you later when another job comes open. A recruiter or hirer may even give you general advice about how to frame your skills, or other jobs that would fit well. Important to note, a recruiter could also give you advice on how to gain the skills you might lack.

You don't have to apply to the job to contact a recruiter. If a recruiter's name is listed with a job opening, you can simply contact them through the website or via email and ask them to tell you more about certain listing points. Like a busy professor, however, a recruiter will be less likely to reply if you ask something such as, "Can you tell me more about this job?" Specific questions are better—for example, "I see the listing includes 'research' as a desired skill. Can you tell me if you are looking for industry-specific research experience or scientific training?"

Some recruiters will respond and be helpful. Those who are willing will continue to help you understand this listing and potentially other job opportunities. This can be an effective way to build an understanding of how certain terms are used in certain industries. This process, along with all the steps in this chapter, will introduce you to the kinds of skills that industries value, and those skills will likely be things you never thought to list on your résumé. It can give you new ideas about how to critically examine the ways you do things, describe the things you've learned that are not in textbooks (the "soft skills" of your work), and find otherwise obscured skills.

As you communicate with more recruiters and hirers, you will find yourself on their lists of candidates for future job openings. You might find yourself 6 months into a search with no leads only to have a recruiter call you with a promising, as-yet-unlisted job opening.

It is also perfectly acceptable at this point to ask the recruiter for advice on your résumé and job search. Even if you are not a fit for a specific job, a good recruiter will take that opportunity to expand their knowledge of the talent pool. A recruiter in an industry that hires researchers and already knows that they should be interested in you may want to look at your résumé and keep your name on file for the future, and may be a rich source of ideas for finding obscured skills.

ADOPT THE RIGHT MIND-SET

Applying for jobs using the steps listed here should help you define the sets of skills needed to pursue careers you're interested in. Whichever of those skills you do not have already or will not get from your graduate training are the ones you need to pursue elsewhere. But, you might ask, aren't people supposed to finish their training before they apply to jobs? Where am I going to find the time to do all this preparation while I'm trying to design and carry out dissertation research?

Our answer to the first question is, often, no. Many undergraduate students complete internships well before they are ready to graduate, and many graduate students in other fields do the same. And for a psychology graduate student, who likely has not received any training or preparation for nonacademic jobs, you might need that job market exposure even more. So we recommend starting this process early.

As for finding the time to build your skills and post iterations of your résumé, we think the time is there in your schedule if you make it. The years you spend in graduate school are meant to be career training. You are preparing for your life's work. If you are interested in a nonacademic career, then your graduate training years are the time to prepare for it. Yes, your department's curriculum is demanding. But adding 1 or 2 hours per week to your workload, especially starting after you've completed the coursework typical of most programs' early years, is entirely feasible and could result in a big payoff.

WRAP-UP

For most behavioral scientists entering the nonacademic workforce, applying for jobs will not be a simple or quick process. It will more likely be a long iterative process, during which a good deal of learning and adaptation will take place. There are probably not many jobs that are *perfect* fits for newly minted psychology PhDs. Recognizing that, and embarking on the process with a deliberate, thoughtful strategy, can help make it more fruitful.

TAKEAWAYS

- Applying for jobs should not be seen as a series of submissions eventually resulting in a job offer.

- Reading job listings can start to reveal skills and roles that you need to develop.

- Iteratively posting résumés and applying for jobs will likely reveal how to frame or present your skills and better match them to job listings.

- Contacting recruiters and hirers could be one of the best ways to understand the skills you lack and how to enhance them, as well as connect with jobs.

References

Achor, S. (2010). *The happiness advantage: The seven principles of positive psychology that fuel success and performance at work*. New York, NY: Crown Business/Random House.

Ansorge, U., Kiss, M., & Eimer, M. (2009). Goal-driven attentional capture by invisible colors: Evidence from event-related potentials. *Psychonomic Bulletin & Review, 16*, 648–653. http://dx.doi.org/10.3758/PBR.16.4.648

Ariely, D. (2010). *Predictably irrational: The hidden forces that shape our decisions*. New York, NY: Harper Perennial.

Biswas, A. K., & Kirchherr, J. (2015). Prof, no one is reading you. *The Straits Times*. Retrieved from https://www.straitstimes.com/opinion/prof-no-one-is-reading-you

Buehler, R., Griffin, D., & Peetz, J. (2010). The planning fallacy: Cognitive, motivational, and social origins. *Advances in Experimental Social Psychology, 43*, 1–62.

Cain, S. (2012). *Quiet: The power of introverts in a world that can't stop talking*. New York, NY: Crown.

Cialdini, R. B. (2006). *Influence: The psychology of persuasion* (Rev. ed.). New York, NY: Harper Business.

Csikszentmihalyi, M. (1990). *Flow: The psychology of optimal experience*. New York, NY: Harper & Row.

Deci, E. L., & Flaste, R. (1996). *Why we do what we do: Understanding self-motivation*. London, England: Penguin.

Duhigg, C. (2012). *The power of habit: Why we do what we do in life and business*. New York, NY: Random House.

Dweck, C. S. (2008). *Mindset: The new psychology of success*. New York, NY: Ballantine Books.

Feibel, C. (2016, September 12). How the 'elevator speech' is gaining traction among scientists. *Here & Now*. Retrieved from http://www.wbur.org/hereandnow/2016/09/12/elevator-pitch-scientists

Friedman, R. (2015). *The best place to work: The art and science of creating an extraordinary workplace*. New York, NY: TarcherPerigree.

Gallagher, P., Fleeson, W., & Hoyle, R. (2011). A self-regulatory mechanism for personality trait stability: Contra-trait effort. *Social Psychological and Personality Science, 2,* 335–342. http://dx.doi.org/10.1177/1948550610390701

Gawronski, B. (2004). Theory-based bias correction in dispositional inference: The fundamental attribution error is dead, long live the correspondence bias. *European Review of Social Psychology, 15,* 183–217. http://dx.doi.org/10.1080/10463280440000026

George, A. (2019, April 9). 3 easy ways to tell your career story on LinkedIn. *The Inc. Life.* Retrieved from https://www.inc.com/amy-george/3-easy-ways-to-tell-your-career-story-on-linkedin.html

Gielan, M. (2015). *Broadcasting happiness: The science of igniting and sustaining positive change.* Dallas, TX: BenBella Books.

Gilbert, D. T. (2006). *Stumbling on happiness.* New York, NY: Knopf.

Gilovich, T., & Ross, L. (2015). *The wisest one in the room: How you can benefit from social psychology's most powerful insights.* New York, NY: Free Press.

Gosling, S. (2008). *Snoop: What your stuff says about you.* New York, NY: Basic Books.

Haidt, J. (2012). *The righteous mind: Why good people are divided by politics and religion.* New York, NY: Pantheon/Random House.

Heath, C., & Heath, D. (2007). *Made to stick: Why some ideas survive and other die.* New York, NY: Random House.

Iyengar, S. (2011). *The art of choosing.* New York, NY: Twelve.

Kahneman, D. (2011). *Thinking, fast and slow.* New York, NY: Farrar, Straus and Giroux.

Kahneman, D., & Miller, D. T. (1986). Norm theory: Comparing reality to its alternatives. *Psychological Review, 93,* 136–153. http://dx.doi.org/10.1037/0033-295X.93.2.136

Keltner, D. (2016). *The power paradox: How we gain and lose influence.* New York, NY: Penguin.

Kolowich, L. (2019, March 29). 17 truly inspiring company vision and mission statement examples. *HubSpot.* Retrieved from https://blog.hubspot.com/marketing/inspiring-company-mission-statements

Langer, E. J. (1989). *Mindfulness.* Reading, PA: Addison-Wesley Longman.

Leary, M. R. (2004). *The curse of the self: Self-awareness, egotism, and the quality of human life.* New York, NY: Oxford University Press. http://dx.doi.org/10.1093/acprof:oso/9780195172423.001.0001

Leary, M. R., Diebels, K. J., Davisson, E. K., Jongman-Sereno, K. P., Isherwood, J. C., Raimi, K. T., . . . Hoyle, R. (2017). Cognitive and interpersonal features of intellectual humility. *Personality and Social Psychology Bulletin, 43,* 793–813.

Lundberg, K. B., & Payne, B. K. (2014). Decisions among the undecided: Implicit attitudes predict future voting behavior of undecided voters. *PLoS One, 9*(1), e85680. http://dx.doi.org/10.1371/journal.pone.0085680

Lyubomirsky, S. (2007). *The how of happiness: A scientific approach to getting the life you want.* New York, NY: Penguin Press.

Markus, H. R., & Conner, A. (2013). *Clash! How to thrive in a multicultural world.* New York, NY: Plume.

Minnesota State CAREERwise. (2012). *What employers are really looking for.* Retrieved from http://careerwise.minnstate.edu/careers/employers-looking. html

National Association of Colleges and Employers. (n.d.). Career readiness defined. Retrieved from https://www.naceweb.org/career-readiness/competencies/ career-readiness-defined/

National Center for Science and Engineering Statistics. (2017, June). *2015 doctorate recipients from U.S. universities* (Report No. NSF 17-306). Arlington, VA: National Science Foundation. Retrieved from https://nsf.gov/statistics/ 2017/nsf17306/static/report/nsf17306.pdf

National Public Radio, & TED. (2016, July 15). What makes us . . . us [Podcast episode]. In G. Raz (Editorial director), *TED radio hour.* Washington, DC: National Public Radio. Retrieved from http://www.npr.org/programs/ ted-radio-hour/485704159/what-makes-us-us

Oppenheimer, D. M. (2008). The secret life of fluency. *Trends in Cognitive Sciences, 12,* 237–241. http://dx.doi.org/10.1016/j.tics.2008.02.014

Pennebaker, J. W. (2011). *The secret life of pronouns: What our words say about us.* New York, NY: Bloomsbury Press.

Pink, D. H. (2009). *Drive: The surprising truth about what motivates us.* New York, NY: Riverhead Books.

Postulate. (n.d.). In *Merriam-Webster.com dictionary.* Retrieved from https:// www.merriam-webster.com/dictionary/postulate

Schuman, R. (2014). "Alt-Ac" to the rescue? *Slate.* Retrieved from https:// slate.com/human-interest/2014/09/a-changing-view-of-alt-ac-jobs-in-which- ph-d-s-work-outside-of-academia.html

Schwartz, B. (2004). *The paradox of choice: Why more is less.* New York, NY: Ecco Press.

Seligman, M. E. P. (2002). *Authentic happiness: Using the new positive psychology to realize your potential for lasting fulfillment.* New York, NY: Free Press.

Seligman, M. E. P. (2006). *Learned optimism: How to change your mind and your life.* New York, NY: Vintage Books.

Seligman, M. E. P. (2013). *Flourish: A visionary new understanding of happiness and well-being.* New York, NY: Free Press.

Shields, J. (2018, September 26). How to write a LinkedIn summary (about section): Examples and tips. *Jobscan blog.* Retrieved from https://www.jobscan.co/ blog/linkedin-summary-examples/

Social Psychology Network. (n.d.). Sources of research funding. Retrieved from https://www.socialpsychology.org/funding.htm

Society for Human Resource Management. (2016, October 11). SHRM/ Mercer findings: Entry-level applicant job skills. Retrieved from https:// www.shrm.org/hr-today/trends-and-forecasting/research-and-surveys/ PublishingImages/Pages/Entry-Level-Applicant-Job-Skills-Survey-/Entry- Level%20Applicant%20Job%20Skills%20Survey.pdf

Soman, D. (2015). *The last mile: Creating social and economic value from behavioral insights*. Toronto, Ontario, Canada: University of Toronto Press.

Thaler, R. H., & Sunstein, C. R. (2009). *Nudge: Improving decisions about health, wealth, and happiness*. New York, NY: Penguin Books.

Tomkins, A., Zhang, M., & Heavlin, W. D. (2017). Reviewer bias in single- versus double-blind peer review. *Proceedings of the National Academy of Sciences of the United States of America*, *114*, 12708–12713. http://dx.doi.org/10.1073/pnas.1707323114

Top Nonprofits. (n.d.). 30 example vision statements. Retrieved from https://topnonprofits.com/examples/vision-statements/

Twenge, J. M. (2006). *Generation me: Why today's young Americans are more confident, assertive, entitled—and more miserable than ever before*. New York, NY: Free Press.

Twenge, J. M., & Campbell, W. K. (2009). *The narcissism epidemic: Living in the age of entitlement*. New York, NY: Free Press.

Urban, J. B., & Linver, M. R. (Eds.). (2019). *Building a career outside academia: A guide for doctoral students in the behavioral and social sciences*. Washington, DC: American Psychological Association. http://dx.doi.org/10.1037/0000110-000

U.S. Department of Health and Human Services. (n.d.). Grant-making agencies. Retrieved from https://www.grants.gov/web/grants/learn-grants/grant-making-agencies.html

Ward, S. (2018, December 24). How to write a mission statement & mission statement examples. *The Balance Small Business*. Retrieved from https://www.thebalancesmb.com/how-to-write-a-mission-statement-2948001

Wilson, T. D. (2015). *Redirect: Changing the stories we live by*. New York, NY: Back Bay Books.

Index

Q

Qualifications, 6, 73, 153
Qualifications-related content, 121–133
  in elevator pitches, 126–129
  in longer descriptive passages,
    129–132
  messaging for, 122–125
  in one-sentence statements, 125–126
Quantitative analysis, careers in,
  152–153

R

Rand Corporation, 142
Rationale, in professional proposals, 89
"Rational" thinking, 32
R&D departments. *See* Research and
    development departments
Recommendations
  impactful, 43–44
  skills for generating, 59–60
Recruiters, 141, 163–165
Rejection of application, 163
Replication crisis, 27, 38
Reputation, 27, 44–47
Required skills, 161, 164–165
Research
  in business settings, 55
  describing specialty of, 54–55
  focusing on purpose of, 41–42
  on job listings, 161
  teaching, to nonscientific audiences, 86
  transferable skills in, 54–58
  use of term, in job listings, 161
Research and development (R&D)
    departments, 72, 103, 150
Research designs, complexity of, 58
Research findings
  applications of, 105–106
  for nonscientific audiences, 87, 95
  premises about evaluation of, 27, 38–39
  simplifying, 80–82
  summarizing, 82–83
Research-focused positions
  at consulting firms, 154
  at contract research organizations, 140
  in industrial/organizational psychology,
    143–144
  at public relations firms, 149
  at think tanks or nonprofits, 143
Research freedom, 57–58

Research methodology
  academic premises about presenting,
    40–42
  value of expertise in, 54, 149–151
Research programs, creating, 57
Research psychologists
  consulting positions for, 153
  entrepreneurship for, 157
  I/O psychology vs. training for, 143, 144
  product development positions for,
    103–104
  in quantitative analysis, 152–153
Résumé(s)
  advice from recruiters on, 164–165
  coalition-building skills on, 72
  and CVs, 53–54
  mission statements on, 110
  posting, to job sites, 161–162
  preparing, for segmented job market, 115
  project management skills on, 70
  revising/varying, 162
  team experience on, 91
  value propositions on, 116–117
  writing your, 63–64
Risk management, 87–88
Risks, in professional proposals, 89

S

Sales-related positions, coalition
    building in, 72
SBDC (Small Business Development
    Center), 77, 129
Schedule, in proposals, 89
Scientific method, premises on, 24, 26
Scientific training, 6
  in academic premises, 24
  and skills required for nonacademic
    positions, 52, 79–92
Scientific writing, 60, 73
Secondary hypotheses, 24, 69–70
The Secret Life of Pronouns (Pennebaker), 83
Segment analysis, 115
Segments, defined, 115
Self-promotion, 117
Self-reflection, 160
Selling and "selling out," 27, 80, 101
Semmelweis, Ignaz, 44
Service Corps of Retired Executives, 77
Seven plus-or-minus two rule, 130
Shields, Jon, 133
Simplicity, 80–83, 125

About the Authors

Patrick Gallagher, PhD, applies behavioral science daily in his position as director of research at the BB&T Leadership Institute. His professional roles in industry have included marketing, customer experience, corporate communications, consulting, and employee engagement. Patrick regularly works with managers and C-suite executives and has been involved in hiring employees with and without psychology backgrounds. He lives in Winston-Salem, NC. Visit https://www.portablephd.com/ and follow @POAtraining on Twitter.

Ashleigh Gallagher, PhD, is senior lecturer and director of undergraduate studies in the Psychology Department at the University of North Carolina at Greensboro. She leads the departmental system for academic advising, as well as the undergraduate internship program. She teaches courses, including an undergraduate course on the career possibilities available to psychology students, and she serves as a faculty teaching mentor to graduate students. She lives in Winston-Salem, NC. Visit https://www.portablephd.com/ and follow @POAtraining on Twitter.

AMERICAN
PSYCHOLOGICAL
ASSOCIATION

Attn: Order Department
P.O. Box 92984
Washington, DC 20090-2984
(800) 374-2721
(202) 336-6123 (TDD)

Bill To: 03092020-4
P.O. # Advance Copy

R. Eric Landrum, PhD
Department of Psychological Science
1910 University Drive
Education Bldg 627, MS 1715
Boise, ID 83725
UNITED STATES

Order # 3920-4

Ship To: 03092020-4
Ship Via: UPS GRD

R. Eric Landrum, PhD
Department of Psychological Science
1910 University Drive
Education Bldg 627, MS 1715
Boise, ID 83725
UNITED STATES

Packing List

GST# R127612802
FEDERAL I.D. NO. 53 020-5890
ALL PRODUCTS MANUFACTURED IN U.S.

Stock #	Title/Description	Qty Ord	Qty B/O	Qty Ship	List Price	Unit Price	Amount
4313057	Portable PhD - Softcover	1	0	1	0.00	0.00	0.00

Item is in Box(es):   Box 1 - 1 pcs

FOR INDIVIDUAL AND INSTITUTION USE ONLY

AMERICAN
PSYCHOLOGICAL
ASSOCIATION

R e t u r n   F o r m

Required Information

*Date:

*Return Number: *(Please Contact APA for Return Number)*

*Returned By:

*Order Number:

*Reason For Return (circle one):   Damaged | Incorrect Item | Other

Comments:

*Quantity	*Item Number	*Description	*Warehouse Use Only*				
			Qty R	Qty RW	Qty N	Qty T	TCOD

AMERICAN
PSYCHOLOGICAL
ASSOCIATION

APA & MAGINATION BOOK ORDER RETURNS

Policy: August 1984 Revised 05/10/10

ALL RETURNS:	• Damages, defects, or shortages must be reported immediately. Claims made 30 days or more following the invoice date will not be honored.
	• Material must be undamaged and in resalable condition.
	• Pamphlets, videos, DVDs, computer software, and CE exams are **not** returnable.
	• Postage on returns is the responsibility of the customer. In the case of APA misshipment or damages, only standard postage/UPS rates will be credited/refunded. For your own protection, please send returns via UPS or other traceable method. Please do not send returns to our 750 First Street, Washington, DC address. **The APA will not be responsible for lost returns without proof of delivery notification or for returns that are from other publishers.**
	• ALL ITEMS MUST BE RETURNED TO:
	APA Returns Department C/O BrightKey, Inc. Suite A 1780 Crossroads Drive Odenton, MD 21113
INDIVIDUALS and INSTITUTIONS: *(Please complete the form provided on the back of this policy and include it with your return)*	• Returns are accepted within 30 days of the invoice date. For APA records please indicate the reason for the return.
	• Enclose a copy of the APA invoice, packing slip, or note the APA invoice or order number in a cover letter. (If unknown, provide complete title information, purchaser's name, address to which order was sent, phone number, and date of purchase).
	• Refunds are made by check or in the case of credit card payment, by crediting your account. Shipping and handling fees are not refundable.
RESELLERS: *(With Returnable Accounts)*	• Written permission is required. For permission to be granted, please provide title and/or APA item number, quantity ordered, invoice and/or purchase order number of original order.
	• Returns must be made within 12 months of the invoice date.
	• All overstock returns must consist of in-print titles only.
	• Please fax or mail your permission request only to:
	APA Returns Department 750 First Street NE Washington, DC 20002 Fax: (202) 336-5502
	• After receiving permission, please package books securely and enclose your "Permission to Return" document with the return. In the case of multiple box returns, each box must be numbered 1 of (total number of boxes) etc. A copy of the "Permission to Return" document must be in each box. Failure to comply could result in an insufficient and/or delayed credit. APA will not be responsible for shortages in credit due to customer's failure to adhere to the return policy.

APA Authorized Distributors:

department will mail a copy of each credit memo to the billing account address. Credit must be used within one year of the credit memo date. Always refer to the credit memo number when deducting and/or corresponding about credit.

- Claims for non-receipt of credit or insufficient credit resulting from a return must be made within 12 months of the return.

Claims for credit submitted after 12 months of a return will not be honored.

Refer to your file copy. To obtain a copy, please call the number below.

APA & MAGINATION BOOK ORDER TERMS OF SALE   Policy: June 1987 Revised 1/02

PAYMENT/INVOICING: All orders must be prepaid unless submitted on a purchase order. Payment is due 30 days from the invoice date.

SHIPPING/HANDLING: Shipping and handling is based on the order total per order or ship to address. See scale below.

Purchases	U.S. & Puerto Rico	Non-U.S. Economy Service	Non-U.S. Guaranteed Service
Up to $14.99	$5.00	$15.00	$50.00
$15.00 - $59.99	$6.00	$16.00	$75.00
$60.00 and Up	10% of Total	$20.00	$125.00

RUSH PROCESSING: Rush processing is available for an additional $10.00 per order, and provides shipment within 2 working days of order receipt.

SHIPMENT METHOD: Routine shipment is by United Parcel Service (UPS) Ground Delivery Service. Allow 7-10 business days for delivery from date the order is received. Shipping methods other than UPS Ground Service are available by request, but will be assessed the charge for the requested method in addition to the shipping and handling fee.

CLAIMS: Damage, shortages, or defective items must be reported immediately upon receipt. Claims made 30 days or more following the invoice date will not be honored.

RETURNS: The APA invoice number is requested. Except for APA error, shipping and handling charges and return shipping cost are not refundable. See RETURNS POLICY for additional terms. Pamphlets, videos, and software programs are not returnable.

Additional Terms for Resellers Only:

PAYMENT/INVOICING: Net 30 days from invoice date.

DISCOUNT: Those purchasing for resale (bookstores, agents, etc.) are entitled to a discount off the list price of applicable titles. Journal back issues are not discounted, except "special issues."

SHIPPING/HANDLING: Actual shipping charges will be added to the invoice except for shipment via trucking company which will be shipped via freight collect. No handling fee will be charged. However, RUSH processing is available at $10.00 per order and provides shipment within 2 working days of receipt of order.

APA-Designated Distributors: Please refer to your distributor agreement or request a copy from an APA Service Representative.

QUESTIONS? CONTACT THE ORDER DEPARTMENT

Phone: 1-800-374-2721 OR (202) 336-5510

Email: order@apa.org

*Customer Signature: ***Date:**

Date Received: _____ Returned by: Cust./Carrier   Via: _____   Correspondence Enclosed: Y / N

Skid Number: _____   Cust. #: _____   RMA #: _____   CM #: _____

Received By: _____   Processed By: _____

Credit Amount: $ _____   Credit For: Book / S&H / Rush Charge / Return Postage

In the form of: Credit Memo / Debit Memo / Refund (Check) / Refund (Credit Card) / Cancel Invoice

Notes:

Return Policy: Videos, computer software, pamphlets, and POD (print-on-demand) merchandise are not returnable. Shipping and Handling charges are not refundable. APA publications may be returned within 30 days of invoice date. Merchandise must be in resalable condition. Please include an original invoice or Packing list along with a brief reason for return. Permission is required for resellers and distributors. Fax your request listing items you wish to return to (202) 336-5502 referencing your P.O. number or your APA invoice number.

PLEASE RETURN MERCHANDISE TO
APA RETURNS DEPARTMENT
c/o BRIGHTKEY
1780 CROSSROADS DRIVE
ODENTON, MD 21113

SHIPPING & HANDLING	0.00
ORDER TOTAL	0.00
PAYMENT RECEIVED	0.00